THE TRUTH

World Mythology in Theory and Everyday Life

Series Editors: Tok Thompson and Gregory Schrempp

This series presents an innovative and accessible overview of the world's mythological traditions. The inaugural volume provides a theoretical introduction to the study of myth, while the individual case studies from throughout time and around the world help guide the reader through the wondrous complexity and diversity of myths, and their widespread influences in human cultures, societies, and everyday lives.

The Truth of Myth: World Mythology in Theory and Everyday Life
Tok Thompson and Gregory Schrempp

THE TRUTH OF MYTH

World Mythology in Theory and Everyday Life

Tok Thompson and Gregory Schrempp

OXFORD
UNIVERSITY PRESS

Oxford University Press is a department of the University of Oxford. It furthers the University's objective of excellence in research, scholarship, and education by publishing worldwide. Oxford is a registered trade mark of Oxford University Press in the UK and certain other countries.

Published in the United States of America by Oxford University Press
198 Madison Avenue, New York, NY 10016, United States of America.

© Oxford University Press 2020

All rights reserved. No part of this publication may be reproduced, stored in a retrieval system, or transmitted, in any form or by any means, without the prior permission in writing of Oxford University Press, or as expressly permitted by law, by license, or under terms agreed with the appropriate reproduction rights organization. Inquiries concerning reproduction outside the scope of the above should be sent to the Rights Department, Oxford University Press, at the address above.

You must not circulate this work in any other form
and you must impose this same condition on any acquirer.

Library of Congress Cataloging-in-Publication Data
Names: Thompson, Tok, author. | Schrempp, Gregory Allen, 1950– author.
Title: The truth of myth : world mythologies in theory and everyday life /
Tok Thompson and Gregory Schrempp.
Description: First edition. | New York : Oxford University Press, 2020. |
Series: World mythology in theory and everyday | Includes
bibliographical references and index.
Identifiers: LCCN 2019039317 (print) | LCCN 2019039318 (ebook) |
ISBN 9780190222789 (hardback) | ISBN 9780190222802 (paperback) |
ISBN 9780197506691 (epub) | ISBN 9780190222796 (updf)
Subjects: LCSH: Mythology. | Manners and customs.
Classification: LCC BL312 .T46 2020 (print) | LCC BL312 (ebook) |
DDC 201/.3—dc23
LC record available at https://lccn.loc.gov/2019039317
LC ebook record available at https://lccn.loc.gov/2019039318

1 3 5 7 9 8 6 4 2

Paperback printed by LSC Communications, United States of America
Hardback printed by Bridgeport National Bindery, Inc., United States of America

CONTENTS

Prologue | vii

Introduction: A World Made of Myth | 1

1. Definitions and Starting Points | 7

2. Highlights in the History of Mythological Research | 37

3. Studying Mythology Comparatively | 99

4. Some Current Trends | 144

Conclusion: Moving Forward with Myth | 178

GLOSSARY | 183
WORKS CITED | 189
INDEX | 197

PROLOGUE

To the student of myth:

This book attempts to provide a concise overview of the theoretical approaches to studying mythology, both in theory and in everyday life.

Whether one is interested in a particular myth or mythic tradition, understanding comparative mythology more broadly, or even the subject and overview of mythology as a whole, this text attempts to present a clear and understandable introduction to some of the best tried-and-true approaches, as well as to address some of the perennial problems and points of confusion.

To embark on the study of myth is to join a noisy chorus of scholars, both present and past, in attempting to divine the meaning of some of the most important, intriguing, and at times puzzling narratives that humankind has ever crafted. We hope this text will help provide you with the theoretical background and tools to allow for a rich, full study of mythology in all its myriad forms.

To the teacher of myth:

Myth has been the source of a great deal of theoretical disagreement and confusion as well. We have tried to address some of the controversies by appealing to a close and careful consideration of the data, which at times helps keep lofty theorizing firmly anchored in the real world. Additionally, we have tried to present an in-depth historical background to the study of myth, which should also help illuminate the close relationships between a society and that society's views of myth. Mythology does not occur without people: it is only with a strong grounding in the study of humankind that we can hope to make progress in our understanding. Where doubt within the scholarly community has arisen, we have tried to pay attention to both sides of the debates. The resulting text is intended to be a detailed, yet engaging, introduction to the study of world mythology, and a scholarly counterweight to popular, unscientific views.

Our experience in teaching myth is that the most vexing issues stem from the several strained if not contradictory connotations that the term "myth" carries. Is myth archaic, or is it part of all societies and thus modern as well? Is it part of religion and/or science, or does it contrast with these? Most vexingly, does "myth" designate falsehood, or the highest forms of truth—those that form the core, guiding principles of particular societies' engagements of the cosmos and life within it? There is also the double signification of the term "mythology," which points to both an academic tradition and the object studied by that tradition. Our view is that while such antinomies are unlikely to be resolved in the foreseeable future, much can be gained by locating and identifying them and by attempting to understand how and why they have emerged. We hope that this approach not only lends clarity to the topic of myth, but also serves to energize the study to which we now turn.

Introduction

A World Made of Myth

Understanding **myth** is a transformative act, a way of grasping the power of culture in one of its most elemental forms. Myths have captivated the worldly-minded for millennia, and are one of the oldest subjects of scholarly inquiry. This book aims to be an intellectual travel guide for scholars, students, and anyone interested in expanding their knowledge of how humans narrate their most fundamental beliefs in strikingly diverse and exotic ways, and attempts to offer assistance in understanding how various peoples create, enact, and narrate myths as ways of establishing core principles regarding the makeup of reality and our place in it.

Doing justice to such a vast topic, with so many divergences as well as commonalities, and so many theoretical aspects and approaches, is a daunting task. Our approach to this task is to seek to provide a useful toolkit for understanding a world of myriad differences. This book, then, does not offer up a unitary or universalist theory, but rather an overview of the many theoretical approaches that have proved useful for advancing scholarship in myth studies around the world. This core text seeks to foster a common vocabulary through which fruitful and productive discussions of myths—whether ancient Aztec or contemporary Hindu—can take place. It is designed to give students of myth, or of any particular mythic tradition, a set of operations and thought processes with which to better understand the role of such fundamental narratives in establishing what to believe, and why. Every discipline of course gives rise to a distinctive terminology; a concluding glossary lists and defines a number of recurrent, key terms in the study of mythology, and the first occurrence of each of these within the text is set in bold.

The title *The Truth of Myth* is a play on words (appropriately enough, in our understanding, since words themselves are culturally created ways of categorizing and understanding reality). The title does not mean we intend to establish once and for all a single way of understanding myth (we do not), nor do we mean to argue that myths are, in any literal sense, necessarily true (definitely not). Rather, the title is a nod to the ways in which, in many societies worldwide, certain narratives are accorded a status that allows them to set the ideological, cultural, and cognitive categories necessary for discussing what is, and what is not, true. Myths not only set about to discuss how the world was created, we will argue, but are also themselves a part of the process of world-making.

The title is also a playful way of opposing a belittling and corrosive use of the term as inherently "false," as in the popular term "urban myth," wherein "myth" is taken as meaning, simply, a widely held falsehood (as in "it's a myth that one is supposed to drink eight glasses of water each day"). Such a definition can be viewed as part and parcel of the cross-cultural difficulties in understanding what myths are, why people have them, and what meanings people draw from them. Other people's myths often seem wildly fantastical, while our own seem pleasantly sensible and soothing. To study myths in a comparative sense, then, is to swim against currents of provincialism, and to realize the fantastic diversity of ways in which our relationship to the universe is conceptualized and narrativized. To learn about others is also, ultimately, to learn about oneself.

Accompanying this core theoretical text is the book series World Mythology in Theory and in Everyday Life, a set of case studies, to explore particular areas, groups, narratives, and topics in myth research. The case studies in this series, intended to grow over time, range through cultures and civilizations including the industrial modern, the contemporary hunter-gatherer, ancient states, and many more.

With myths exhibiting such striking divergences, understanding myths in general must go hand in hand with understanding myths in particular. We thus offer the reader this core theoretical text as a toolkit and travel guide to be utilized in the exploration of a wide range of specific traditions. It is hoped that this combination, the theoretical along with specific mythological traditions that impinge on the everyday lives of peoples, will help sketch the vast contours of myth on planet earth in a way that becomes understandable to the outsider, the foreigner, the student, the traveler. One might, for example, wish to combine the theoretical text with any one or number of case studies, both to avail of the various approaches, as well as to understand more widely the commonalities and divergences in myths around the world.

There is a strong need for such a sober, scholarly, and investigative approach to myth studies: in spite of a rich intellectual background in the study of myth, there is a vast misunderstanding and ignorance of what myths are, and what people do with them. Partly, this is due to a sort of magical power of the term "myth," which sometimes attracts myth-making more than myth explication. Popular accounts often overgeneralize about mythology, without considering all the detailed specificities of various mythic traditions around the world. Partly, this is also due to the constraints of area experts in mythology—people may spend their whole lives studying one mythological tradition, without always understanding how it compares and contrasts to other traditions. To do the topic justice, then, requires an approach that will include both specialization and generalization, both in-depth knowledge of a particular language and culture, as well as knowledge of myth and myth studies worldwide.

We attempt to achieve an inclusion of both perspectives, first in this core text, *The Truth of Myth*, and second in detailing various theoretical approaches to mythologies in conjunction with the individual case studies in the series World Mythology in Theory and Everyday Life, where we dive into particular myths, peoples, and topics. It is hoped that a university course on Norse culture might, for example, include a case study on Norse mythology, along with this core theoretical text. The series will bring together some of the foremost scholars in the world detailing their specific areas of expertise, allowing a rich and full accounting of the traditions, conceptually anchored together in a shared theoretical outlook.

This book and series arose from discussions with colleagues and with editors at Oxford University Press, centering on the problem of reconciling the twin goals of offering useful generalizations while also providing analyses that do justice to the richness and uniqueness of particular mythological traditions. While the scope and size of the subject matter might seem daunting, we are committed to presenting the material in a manner that is approachable, readable, and comprehensible.

We begin by setting out useful definitions and starting points for discussion. While these are always debatable and contestable, we hold that a standard, scholarly, and accepted usage of myth as a particularly profound, formative, and meaningful narrative is both internally consistent and useful. As in the exegesis of the title, we do not mean to imply that our words make it true; rather, we argue that definitions are important, since these are the building blocks, the atoms, of the more complex theoretical applications and approaches. In doing so, we acknowledge both the uses and limitations of language, and the uses and limitations of our own approaches. Rather than trying to establish an "ultimate" definition, we strive to utilize definitions for further purposes, much in the way that we approach the study of myths themselves. Words—especially those that convey definitions—are perhaps the most important tools in our theoretical toolkit, and this means we always need to be critically and reflexively aware of the implications of the language that we are using.

After initial definitions and discussions, we begin our more substantive discussions of what myth is, why people have myth, and what they do with myth. Here, too, we emphasize not some transcendent qualities of these stories, but more the reverse: a sustained acknowledgment that myths do not exist outside of human life. Myths do not "explain" the **cosmos**, or "do" anything at all: people, and only people, enact myths, perform myths, and do things with myths. The focus on "everyday life" in the series is a reminder that myths are a part of everyday life, not something apart from it. And it is clear that they play a large part in everyday life for many if not most people. People do a great many things with myth, and the resulting impact in multiple, ever-changing cultural and social configurations, and in billions of individual lives, is one of the most resplendent and awe-inspiring aspects of this field of study.

The study of mythology has its own origin stories, of course (as do all academic disciplines). Many of these continue to inform contemporary scholarly approaches, some as valuable guides or outlooks, while others serve as more cautionary **tales**. Some of the widely used terms date back to the Classical realm of the Greeks and Romans, while others were introduced at various points along the way, from a variety of cultures and time periods. *The Truth of Myth* gives an overview of the development of the scholarly study of myth, from its earliest times to its most contemporary. In doing so, this study is contextualized within a diachronic theoretical discussion that has been ongoing for millennia and continues to yield new and at times surprising insights.

As with many academic disciplines, the data set for mythological studies has vastly improved in recent years. While early scholars had to rely on distant and dubious accounts of exotic mythologies from foreign lands or ancient civilizations, modern ethnographic research has continued to flourish in many parts of the world, providing for an increasingly rich collection of finely detailed mythographic case studies, helping us to understand myths in their performative contexts. Such linguistically and ethnographically informed work allows us to deepen our understanding of why and how myths continue to be such an important part of cultural **worldviews**, and to witness the diverse and moving ways in which people perform them. Accordingly, this study presents an overview and (re-)assessment of some of the nuanced ways that people engage with mythic narratives.

Myths can unite great numbers of people, concepts, or ideas: they can also divide them. In our core text, we examine some of the common dichotomies and oppositions employed in discussing myth (for example, one often hears of myth versus science, myth versus truth, or myth versus religion). Dichotomies can reveal important linguistic dialogues that seek to define particular views, for particular reasons. Therefore, studying these contested meanings helps us understand in detail the various paths people take toward understanding the topic of mythology, generally, as well as the role of mythology in their own (including scholarly) lives.

Myths are an important, dynamic, and complex part of being human, revealing a great deal of global cultural diversity. Myths help to categorize fundamental properties of the cosmos, creating a sense of truth: proper and appropriate categories, questions, and meanings. It is hoped that this book, along with the accompanying series, will help illuminate the complexity, subtlety, and power of humanity's most profound stories, offering a comprehensive view of the many perspectives and theories available to the aspiring mythologist.

Chapter 1

Definitions and Starting Points

A Core Definition

Throughout this work, we will employ a definition of "myth" that we believe most scholarly usages point toward or at least overlap with: myths are narratives of profound cultural and individual importance that in some way help establish our symbolic sense of the ultimate shape and meaning of existence—of ourselves, of everything else in the cosmos, and perhaps especially of the relationship between the two.

Toward elaborating this definition, let's take a closer look at the idea of narrative. The word "narrative" is, in various versions, employed in many European languages, particularly of the Romance family. The word has been traced by etymologists as far back as the Sanskrit *gna*, to "know," and it can be followed through the influence of Latin, in which it bifurcates into two words: "knowing" (*gnarus*), and "telling" (*narro*). It is interesting that the very root word of "knowing" was related to "telling"—knowledge is a social process, requiring both a performer and an audience; both listening, and relating. The "telling" aspect becomes further solidified with

7

"storytelling" by the late Latin phase of the word, and even more so in the early French phase.

In the American English common usage in the early 2000s, the word "narrative" refers to a communicative genre in which a series of temporally linked events are connected in a diachronic, causal syntax: or, what's usually called a "story." Yet, we could still tease out differences between the two: one can narrate an ongoing series of events, such as a sports broadcaster describing an ongoing sports game, or news broadcaster describing live emergency events as they happen; but these are not "stories," at least not yet.

To be a story implies a narration set in a time *other than* that of the performance. Storytelling may be one of the most important aspects of human culture, allowing us to pass on knowledge from one generation to the next, building, over time, a vast repertoire of narrative knowledge. Most of what we think we are comes from stories: stories of our families, or our tribe, or nation, or religion, or even our own autobiographical stories that we tell ourselves. Stories, more than anything else, give us a sense of identity.

The story may even be a rare example of "humaniqueness." The general scientific consensus from animal studies is that many nonhuman animals can be said to have culture, demonstrated in socially learned, complex behaviors. Increasingly, animal communications are looking complex, and often socially constructed and shared. It has been suggested that nonhuman animals commonly also narrate, especially in terms of warning communications, although, as of yet, storytelling remains demonstrated within the realm of humanity alone. Jack Niles, for instance, published a book entitled *Homo Narrans: The Poetics and Anthropology of Oral Literature*, in which he asserted that "storytelling is an ability that defines the human species as such" (1999, 3). If true, this may provide an important clue to help explain the remarkable success of humankind. Stories, it may be argued, are what make us human more than anything else.

Stories *are* our origin, in this sense, at least. As Pierre Janet stated in his 1928 *L'Evolution de la mémoire et la notion de temps:* "narration created humanity" (261).

We could have reasonably defined myth as "stories," yet we chose the word "narrative" instead. This is in part because of the strong link between the stories and the act of relating them, the process of narration. Often, myths are performed in special contexts, where time and the **sacred** conceptually lessen the distance between the everyday life and that of the mythic: myths are often enacted in **rituals**. This sense of "narration," therefore, is just a bit broader than "story"; and as more suggestive of performance, "narration" more fully does justice to the many ways that myths are related.

This definition is already a stricter one than some employ, and indeed some eminent scholars have sought to expand the use of the term beyond the narrative. For example, Roland Barthes sought to move from narrative to images and ideas, while Henry Glassie has persuasively argued that in some cases sacred material culture can be the center of narratives, rather than the other way around (e.g., Glassie 2002). There may be some efficacy in such expanded views, and our definition is not meant to deny other applications, but rather to focus on a "handy approach" that is specific enough to winnow out "all things are myths" approaches, but general enough to apply across all cultures and mythic traditions. There is a danger in adopting too broad a definition: if a word means everything, then it means nothing. For the purposes of a general introduction to mythology, then, we hold that our definition is a productive limitation. In general, and sufficient for our initial purposes, myths can be productively defined as narratives of particularly profound, symbolic importance, helping to establish our understanding of ourselves and our place in the cosmos.

One of our tasks is to locate the means of transmission of the story: is it performed live, or written in a canonized account?

Writing

Writing can transform stories, perhaps especially when presented in canonized and sacralized forms, as in "holy scripts." Writing can attain a level of fixity uncharacteristic of traditions of live performances (which is to say, in **folklore**).

Scribes producing written Scripture have long shaped Western notions of the inherent link between writing and the sacred. In Christendom, to be a scribe was to be literate, and a member of the Church; to learn to read and write was to become closer to God. Writing and reading is the form of performance most singularly associated with mythology for Abrahamic religions.

The interpretation of sacred texts can, of course, change over time, yet there remain strong attachments to the idea of an unchanging textual narrative. Pyysiäinen (1999) argues that this creates various interpretive groups: priesthoods, theological schools, sects, and various denominations are all engendered by the joint process of agreeing on a core text (the "word of God"), while being able to support different interpretations of that text. In many ways, reliance on a canonized sacred text or texts tends to create much of what we think of as a religion: organized groups and institutions based around beliefs in a particular cosmological view.

Yet writing is not a prerequisite for religion: there are many religions not based on a particular text or texts, and many more (e.g., Hinduism), where there is no one central text. Some traditions may have had their myths written down, but still place importance on oral, performative traditions. *Writing* is deeply connected to the sacred for some groups, and viewed as a purely mundane practice in others.

Even in societies stressing an organized religion based around a particular sacred text, the interpretation of that text can vary widely, creating different ideas of the textual myth. Many times, this is a folk practice, an example of vernacular religion. For example, consider the widespread stories of Lilith, Adam's first wife, which does not appear in the Bible, yet is told as part of the sacred narrative for many groups. Or consider the common representation of the Fruit of Knowledge as an apple—a motif that has no textual recommendation, yet has become a standard part of the story for many people.

For many traditions, writing plays a much smaller role, or no role whatsoever. Indeed, since mythology clearly predates writing as a practice, it's safe to assert that most mythologies have been formed outside of literary influences, through the repetition of countless live performances of storytelling, changing and adapting, emerging and disappearing, for untold passages of time. This is the realm of folklore.

Myth, Mythology, Mythos, Mythography

At this point it is important to note that the root term "myth" appears in several variations. To repeat, we use the term myth to mean a narrative of profound cultural and individual importance that in some ways helps establish our symbolic sense of the ultimate shape and meaning of existence. The related term "mythology" has two uses which are sometimes confused with one-another. In the first usage, "mythology" largely overlaps with "myth," but adds a plural or collective connotation, typically implying the full set of mythic narratives possessed by a particular society (for example, Greek mythology), or sometimes the full set of narratives that have grown up around a particular mythic character (for example, Coyote mythology). But "mythology" can also be used to refer to the *study of* such narratives; hence we use the term "mythology" to label the academic discipline that studies myths/mythology, while the practitioner in this discipline is a mythologist. As alternatives to the term "myth," writers in English sometimes adopt the more direct transliterations of "muthos" or "mythos." "Mythos" sometimes carries the connotation of something like a mystique, mindset, or worldview. For example, the phrase "the mythos of the smartphone" might suggest the set of stories, but also the attitudes, aspirations, and forms of interaction that have grown up around this bit of technology.

Finally, we have the term "mythography," which, in parallel with "mythology," divides into two usages. In the first usage, mythography is the "telling" of myths specifically *through the medium of writing*, and the mythographer is the teller who passes myths on in writing. In the second usage, mythography is *writing about* myths and the mythographer is the commentator who writes about myths. Some literary works are inspired by both goals—telling myths and commenting on them—thus combining the two usages. The terms "mythography" and "mythographer" have gained popularity in recent decades, promoted by scholars who want to emphasize distinctive characteristics of myth/mythology when carried on through writing. There is no reciprocal term to clearly distinguish myth/mythology carried on through oral transmission from myth/mythology carried on through writing, although the default for many scholars is to assume that "myth" (and also "mythology" when referring to narratives, as opposed to the study of narratives) implies that we are dealing with narratives that are, or at least originally were, oral in creation and transmission.

Definition by Contrast, Part One: Storytelling Genres

In folklore studies, stories are commonly divided into three categories: **legends**, myths, and tales. This is, of course, a heuristic device: stories do not come neatly labeled by categories; rather, scholars find that there are useful general distinctions in different types of stories. It is also a device that most certainly emanated from Western culture. Not only is this a tripartite scheme (for more on the importance of three in Western culture, generally, see Dundes [1968]), but it is one that emerges from Western narrative traditions. Other cultures often have their own distinctive categories for narratives (see Bascom 1954), which may, or may not, fit well within these categories. But whatever the provenance, these generic categories, linked with the English language, continue to prove useful, and hence will be employed throughout this book.

Truthiness

The distinctions among these genres can be broken down in several ways, and the notion of "truth" in myths plays a key role in understanding the distinctions. One way of breaking down the various folkloric genres is to look at the "truth value" of the three. Accordingly, we can present the following scheme:

> LEGENDS: plausible, possibly true
> TALES: not true, fictional
> MYTHS: symbolic truth, and, for some, literal truth

Some people believe in a literal Garden of Eden, for example, or may hold that the Rainbow Serpent really did create the landscape of Australia, but literal belief is not the only basis on which people can assent to the visions and lessons offered in myth. The idea of symbolic truth is that the importance of the story is not so much in what happened, but what the narrated scenario *means*. For example, people take various lessons from the Garden of Eden story—regarding gender, mortality, sinfulness, etc.—that they can then apply to their everyday lives, and similarly so with the stories of the Rainbow Serpent. So, *whether or not* people believe that myths are literally true, they may derive profound symbolic importance from the details of the narrative, and this is part of what gives myths their particular moral and rhetorical power.

Myths help us to place our identity vis-à-vis the wider cosmos, and help answer the "big questions": Why was the earth created? Why am I here? What is it to do the right thing? What is my place in the greater schemes of history, and of the cosmos itself? Why do we get married? Why do we die?

Legends, by contrast, are more often directly connected to literal belief. In her magnum opus, the folklorist Linda Dégh (1920–2014) defined legend as a story that "entertains debate about belief" (2001, 97). Legends are told regarding this world, and are held to be possibly true. Many legends are firmly believed by those who relate them, while others may be told in pure disbelief, but allowing that someone else might possibly believe them. Accordingly, legends always occur in this world: the real, mundane, non-sacred world. The frame is geographical more than cosmological.

Legends invite themselves to be proved or disproved, believed or not believed, while myths are used to shape the very foundational categories of the world itself: myths set the stage for what is to be believed, or not. Legends often concern *literal* belief, whereas myths often emphasize *symbolic* belief. Legends often interact with our daily lives: family stories passed down, haunted houses on the edge of town, whereas if and when the mythic touches the mundane, what we have is a *miracle*, a rare and wondrous event, full of import.

Legends are generally thought of as discussing *secular* rather than sacred beliefs, although the two may at times run close together. For example, there are many medieval tales of "Saint's legends" marking the miraculous deeds of Christian saints. For the most part, these are set in the real world, and meant to be believed, yet clearly invoke sacred beliefs as well.

There is much to show that our categories of myths and legends can come close to one another in certain examples. We find many other systems that collapse the two genres of myth and legend altogether, a macro-category of "true" stories versus the fictional stories of tales (see Mould 2002). This serves as a reminder that such categorizations are linguistic and cultural constructions, rather than a discovery of some transcendent truth.

One other important oral narrative genre, **epic**, should be mentioned, and can be described in terms of two of the three main genres already discussed. One subcategory of legend is the "historical legend," that is, narratives about extraordinary humans and their achievements set in the historical past of our present world. An epic might be described as a historical legend that has been raised to a major work of verbal artistry through expanded length and detail as well as poetic form and meter—as in Homer's *Iliad* and *Odyssey* and Vergil's *Aeneid*. While historical legend furnishes the core narrative of these epics, mythology is also relevant, for allusions to the gods and their influence provide a continuous backdrop as the actions of epic **heroes** unfold. Further, such stories often provide for "national mythologies," sacred origin stories of a people, as in the formation of Greek nationhood.

Myths can be perhaps most easily contrasted with "tales." Folklorists often call this genre by the German term *"Märchen,"* since the word "tales" is often used loosely in English. In English, *Märchen* are sometimes referred to as "fairy tales," but this is confusing: most tales do not have fairies, and those European stories in which fairies do appear are most often legends (set in the real world, and told as possibly true, as in, for example, the analogous ghost stories). Tales are fiction, told for reasons other than establishing or discussing truth. Tales are often told for entertainment, and, free from the requirements of believability, are often some of our most fantastical stories. Talking animals, flying carpets, and magic bean seeds are part and parcel for this genre: the realm of the tale can easily include all sorts of wonders. Many tales are humorous. Many are told for pedagogical reasons, especially for children (the English term "nursery tales" applies to this subgenre). Aesop's fables, Grimm's Fairy Tales, and "tall tales" of all varieties do not attempt to establish belief, but rather enrich the everyday linguistic, cultural, and narrative realm of humanity in other ways.

Timeliness

Another (and, again, common) scheme is to group narratives on the basis of the time in which the action is set:

> LEGENDS: in the real, historical world
> TALES: in a fictional world of no particular time ("once upon a time")
> MYTHS: before or at the formation of the world, after or at the end of the world, or posing eternal principles that infuse but also transcend human history

Normally, myths are "before" the real world, and "mythic time" is the time before the world as it is now. This temporal placement allows myths to function as formative stories, and as charters for everyday life. In explaining how things came to be, myths offer guidelines to categorizing and understanding the world, as well as imbuing the world with a sense of meaning, and often morality. Occasionally, we also find myths set at the end of the world, as in the Norse Ragnarok, or the Christian Apocalypse. Also, we may occasionally find myths that appear in a sort of parallel time to our own, overlapping in times of ritual and sacred importance, as in the Australian Dreamtime. In general, though, myths are foundational stories of creation. We find mythic time most often employed in the stories of the world before this one, and how things came to be. Mythic time connects directly to the sacred, the **numinous**, and the very, very important.

Stories of the creation of our cosmos, planet, and species are perhaps some of the most straightforward manifestations of myth, although we acknowledge that many traditions have other spatio-temporal aspects as well. And mythic time itself can run differently to our own temporality: myths can at times be said to be outside of our world, with numinous events transpiring on a different temporal plane than that of earth. In Australian **cosmology**, for example, the Dreamtime is the mythic time in which the landscape itself was shaped, but it is also held to be ongoing in a transcendent manner.

Such temporal recursion, in which the beginning of the world is reunited with our present moment, can be brought forth by active agents, particularly in sacred rituals. The Dreamtime is an explicit example, but this sort of logic often pervades the raison d'être of many of our most sacred rituals: myths can connect the mundane with the sacred, and give meaning to our lives and actions. Myths happen long ago, but do so in a way that is continually echoing in our contemporary lives.

To recap, both truth and time are invoked together in categorizing myth as a genre. In our terminology, we can generally distinguish myths from legends by the general place and time in which these stories are set. Legends are set in our world, the real word, while myths are often narrations of creation—of the cosmos, of the earth, of people, and of many of the aspects of our culture. It is their formative nature that gives myths their symbolic power. They are stories not of how things might be (as are legends), but rather how and why things came to be as they are now.

For our introductory purposes, then, we can say that while legends are placed in our everyday world, myths occur either before, after, or outside of our everyday realm, and are critical to the formation of this realm.

Definition by Contrast, Part Two: Two Troubling Dichotomies

As implied in the foregoing, the meanings and definitions of terms tend to be established through relationships, at once connective and contrastive, with other terms. In the case of "myth," there are at least two major levels on which such relationships are encountered. As just discussed, "myth" on one level connects and contrasts with other genres of oral narrative, including legend, and tale (or "folktale"). But on another level, the notion of "myth" or "mythology" is used to label something like a "worldview," that is, an overall attitude toward or way of understanding the cosmos. Used in this way, "myth" is often paired and contrasted with other terms that also designate such overall attitudes and understandings of the cosmos—and most important, with the terms "religion" and "science." Myth vs. religion, and myth vs. science, are two connective/contrastive pairings that are frequently encountered and also very problematic. Here we will consider what motivates and is involved in these two pairings.

Myth vs. religion

While occasionally one encounters authors who use the terms "mythology" and "religion" interchangeably, more often "mythology" and "religion" are paired in one of two ways: either mythology means religion that is in some way *distant*; or else it refers to a specific *component* of religion. The first of these pairings is problematic and sometimes prejudicial; the second is less problematic and has much to recommend it. Let us consider these two pairings in more detail.

The first pairing, again, draws a distinction between religion and *distant* religion. Distant in what way? Often in such a way that the investigator, by calling it a myth, is indicating that he or she is not a believer in a particular narrative's religious claims but is studying it, rather, for some nonreligious value, such as its sociopolitical significance, aesthetic appeal, psychological or moral insight, or sheer exoticism. There seems to be an inclination to apply the term mythology to religions that are said to be *dead*, that is, no longer supported by a community of believers. "Mythology" is often taught in departments of literature, a disciplinary classification that would seem to emphasize artistic over metaphysical and ritual importance. On the positive side, such a classification might simply voice an honest admission that we no longer share the original ritual and religious worldview of such stories, so we approach them with an eye toward other qualities that we now can more fully appreciate, such as their aesthetic richness or psychological and moral insight.

But it is not just "dead" religions that attract the term mythology, for living religions that are exotic—that is, culturally alien to the scholar or student—can also motivate the "mythology" label. In the case of dead religions, most likely no one is there to object, but in cases in which the religion in question is not dead but merely distant from the scholar's or student's cultural frame, the label of "mythology" can be offensive to a community of religious believers. For the latter, the metaphysical claims and ritual contexts of stories may be more important than the aesthetic, moral, and psychological appeal of those stories. However respectfully approached, the label of "mythology" may be perceived as a diminution if it is understood as implying that the matter at hand is mythology *rather than* religion. Students of mythology should thus be mindful of the pitfall of the term "mythology" when it is used, either blatantly or subtly, to differentiate religion from *distant* religion. At its worst, this dichotomy can amount to the prejudice that spiritual/metaphysical beliefs are religion when they are *mine*, but mythology when they are *yours*.

But there is a second way in which the terms "religion" and "mythology" are paired, and in this one all, or at least most, religions would be seen as containing mythologies. In this second conceptualization, mythology refers to the foundational narratives of a particular religion. Religions typically comprise many different components: doctrines, rules of observance, rituals, incantations, functionaries, perhaps sub-cults and sects, and, yes, stories. The stories associated with a religious tradition may be of many kinds—legends, anecdotes, epics, and so on—but some will likely be myths. Myths are common and ubiquitous in religions. This is not at all to say that "all religions are myths" (religion includes many things besides myths), but rather that there is a strong link between religion and mythology: most if not all religions appear to employ myths in their service. Some scholars may even use the term "myth" or "mythology" as an umbrella term to label the entire narrative component of a particular religion. Whether restricted to one type of narrative or used as an umbrella term, this way of conceptualizing the relation of myth and religion—that the former is one *part* of the latter—has much to recommend it, and is consistent with the approach offered in this book.

There are a number, indeed perhaps an increasing number, of secular phenomena that, like religions, comprise a complex of different components. Consider, for example, the Graceland phenomenon, which involves a shrine, pilgrimages, supernatural sightings, and many types of stories, including those of the culture-hero, Elvis—all of which might lead some to invoke the term "mythology" and at least the term "cult" if not "religion." How important is the criterion of "sacred" to the definition of myth? While some scholars would insist on upholding this criterion—a myth is a *sacred* story—we have opted for the broader criteria of stories that have a "profound" character for societies and individuals. But even if one wants to hold firm on the sacredness criterion, it still would seem necessary to acknowledge that there are secular movements in which myth-like stories form parts of religion-like complexes.

Myth vs. science

The pairing of myth vs. science takes a different form, but certainly is no less complicated, than the pairing of myth vs. religion. Rationalistic philosophers of the eighteenth century (the era of so-called Enlightenment) as well as many scientists today portray the relationship between myth and science as essentially antagonistic: science gradually replaces mythology's false teachings about nature with the truths discovered by science. But there are interesting exceptions to this "zero-sum" rendering: the eminent Harvard biologist E. O. Wilson, for example, says that science will provide humanity with a "new mythos":

The true evolutionary epic, retold as poetry, is as intrinsically ennobling as any religious epic. Material reality discovered by science already possesses more content and grandeur than all religious cosmologies combined. (Wilson 1998, 265)

In calling it a "new mythos" (in contrast with the *old* mythos of religion), Wilson implies that there is a mythic quality in science itself: myth and science are different but also similar. The larger context of Wilson's comment suggests a conviction that science and its findings can provide a motivating spirit capable of energizing and integrating human life, making it coherent, profound, beautiful, and beneficent—functions that scholars of traditional, religiously based mythologies continually discover throughout the world.

We can add much more regarding the common ground occupied by the enterprises that we respectively term science or myth. Both myth and science spring from human fascination with the cosmos and our place in it, and both have a special fascination with the various periodicities found in nature. Both involve observation, wonder, and speculation. Both strive to systematize the myriad details of the cosmos under integrative principles, whether the cosmic genealogies descending from primal Sky/Earth parents in some traditional myths, or the principle of universal gravitation as formulated by Isaac Newton. There are expert mythic storytellers and expert scientists, and both kinds of experts attract admiring audiences. Scientists are people, and people are always influenced by myth, whether indirectly or directly. Finally, although the term "myth" is sometimes used to imply a spirit of pure fantasy, an utter indifference to empirical reality, most mythologies carry a sense of accountability: like science, they want to provide glimpses into what the cosmos actually is and how it really works. What does this leave regarding the *differences* between myth and science? The following is a list of some of the qualities associated more readily with one or the other:

Myth:
    narrative (i.e., storytelling) exposition
    nature viewed as working through personal forces
        (**animism, anthropomorphism**)
    heroes who found the moral values of a society
    an aura of the numinous or sacred

Science:
    logical or argumentative exposition
    nature viewed materialistically and as working through
        impersonal laws
    structured experimentation
    mathematical methods and models

While diverging tendencies are evident, however, none of the qualities listed above would seem to belong exclusively to either myth or science. For example, while stories from traditional mythologies do not often involve mathematical calculus or logarithms, they often do reflect a fascination with quantities and periodicities—the sort of tangible mathematics evident in the workings of nature. Measurements taken in scientific lab-work may be carried out with cold precision, but at other moments scientists will wax poetic and speak in quasi-sacred tones about the sheer wonder of the natural world. With the large and growing impact of science on human life, a vast network of science journalists and popular expositors has arisen; and these science interpreters very often draw on mythic strategies to make science interesting and appealing to a nonspecialized broader audience. They will present the "story" of science, draw upon anthropomorphic metaphors (e.g., the "birth" of the cosmos, the "family" of planets, the "selfish gene"), and accord great scientists the stature of mythic heroes who transform human life and exemplify our noblest values.

The scientifically inspired cosmic visions offered by science popularizers can be quite extravagant. Consider, for example, a futuristic vision offered by the legendary scientist and popular science writer/commentator Carl Sagan, in his book *Pale Blue Dot*. In this work, Sagan prophesies a human diaspora from earth to other habitable planets. Sometime in the future our descendants will recall their Earth-origin, and

> gaze up and strain to find the blue dot in their skies. They will love it no less for its obscurity and fragility. They will marvel at how vulnerable the repository of all our potential once was, how perilous our infancy, how humble our beginnings, how many rivers we had to cross before we found our way. (Sagan 1994, 405)

Interestingly, Sagan opens this same book by reflecting on ideas that the pursuit of scientific knowledge requires us to give up. Prominent in his discussion is the Copernican revolution, or the discovery that the earth is not the center of the solar system or of the universe—the sort of conceptualization that many scientists regard as epitomizing the mythological self-infatuation that science must try to dislodge. But note how Sagan's futuristic vision offers his readers a compensatory vision, a new way to think of the earth as cosmic center. Though no longer the center of the solar system or of some absolute cosmic space, the pale blue dot will be the takeoff point for a cosmic diaspora, a source to which our descendants will forever look back from the surrounding cosmos. Like the many traditional origin myths that portray the cosmos as a family of beings begotten by Father Sky and Mother Earth, Sagan's futuristic vision offers a cosmos, or at least a cosmic region, held together by kinship. Earth as cosmic center, and kinship as cosmic glue: Sagan thus manages to recapture for scientific cosmology two powerful conceits at the core of many "pre-Copernican" mythological cosmologies.

Some will continue to argue, as did the philosophers of the Enlightenment, that the relationship between science and myth is essentially one of displacement: science requires us to leave myth behind. But the work of contemporary popular science expositors, many of whom (including the two mentioned above, E. O. Wilson and Carl Sagan) are themselves accomplished scientists, suggests another possible way of thinking about the relationship: that science and its findings, to become humanly meaningful and appealing, must be continuously re-mythologized—thus, that the relationship of mythology and science is not of displacement so much as one of co-evolution.

Myths Create the World

When we speak of the creation of the world, we could just as easily be referring to either of two things: the physical world that we inhabit, or the social/cultural world in which we live according to the rules, ideas, and technologies that define our particular society. Stories about the ultimate origins of our physical world—at least its overall configuration, its macrostructure—are often easily classified as myths (although colorful stories about particular details, such as why a leopard has spots, might sometimes be referred to by other genre terms such as aetiological tale or even fable). When it comes to our sociocultural world, we face the already-mentioned problem of distinguishing between myth and legend. Stories that celebrate the political and military contributions and achievements of a particular real-world hero are more likely to take the form of legends or epics, while stories about the ultimate, most profound principles at the base of social/cultural existence in general, or at the base of one particular society or kind of society, are typically called myths. Sometimes stories of the creation of the two realms—the physical cosmos and the sociocultural order—are closely correlated, with the later a sort of emanation or echo of the former. For example, in his poem *Theogony*, the Greek poet Hesiod opens with the creation of the physical cosmos of land, sky, and sea, and ends with Zeus' creation of the political regime that organizes the gods. The processes by which Zeus organizes the society of gods parallel many of the processes through which physical cosmos was created, and, further, it is clear that the portrayal of Zeus' reign is intended to provide political models to be followed by the human rulers of Hesiod's own time.

Myths might focus on origins of the landscape, lineage systems, political systems, gender, or death. Myths might detail the origins of fire, or marriage, of sex or the incest **taboo**, of the sun and moon, or, really, just about any other aspect of our world and identity. Myths that detail the origin of the cosmos itself are known as **cosmogonic**, and such narratives have a large representation in our discussion of mythology. "Cosmogonic," properly, refers to the origins of everything—the cosmos. These initial "forming of the cosmos" stories are often so important, so profound, and so symbolic, that other stories likely to be labeled as "myths" can often be seen as emanating from or emerging in parallel with the cosmogonic myths—as in the Hesiodic portrayal just mentioned. The sacred notions attached to such cosmogonic myths make such narratives examples of myths par excellence, and provide a very handy reference to use.

Yet, not all traditions focus their narrative practices on the creation of the universe. For example, Bantu myths frequently portray the universe as eternal, and the focus for many of them is instead the creation of the humans and the lineages that provide the main elements of Bantu social structure. Or one could consider the mythic weight given to "saint's stories" in Ireland, which celebrate the introduction of Christianity to an already well-established land.

In popular political or nationalistic discourse, "myth" often carries a debunking connotation: the incident or event in question did not really happen, or the ideas being promulgated are propaganda. Other usages of the term, however, are more positive or at least ambivalent. To say, for example, that a particular historical event or feat is "of mythic proportions," or that an important historical personage has "entered the realm of myth," is often intended less as a debunking than as the opposite—specifically as an expression of the belief or desire that some moments and actors in history have a transcendent quality, deserving to be raised above the prosaic run of events and held up as timeless guiding examples.

And there is another popular sense, one that is less political than cultural, in which "myth" is sometimes connected with nation. A review by Lisa Kennedy (2008) of the writer-director Paul Thomas Anderson's film *There Will Be Blood* (2007) is titled "'Blood' Hits Gusher of American Myth"; and this is only one of many reviews of this film to invoke the term "myth." The film is about early oil prospecting and drilling in California. At points, the unique personalities of the two protagonists—a preacher and oil prospector—dissolve into grotesque caricatures of two "titanic" forces in American society: religion and money. A stark, empty landscape provides the arena in which these elemental, world-shaping forces face off. There are numerous Hollywood renditions of familiar stories recognized as stemming from Greek, Roman, or biblical mythology; what is interesting about "Blood" is that while not a close rendition of a particular story from any of these traditions, many reviewers yet perceive the film to have a mythic quality. In such examples, we can see how contemporary stories are employed in portraying or reflecting the most foundational forces that shape a certain kind of civilization—if not the primordial physical cosmos, then at least the present-day moral cosmos.

Stories don't come marked as myths, legends, or tales. Rather, our exercise in genre definitions is an attempt to tease out how people who participate in these stories view them: are they considered sacred? Literally true? Told for fun? This is an important point, since the same narrative could conceivably be perceived in any of these genres, depending on the mindset of the participants in the storytelling event. A story that is a fun fiction for one person might be a sacred story to the next, and might be rather a question of factual belief for a third. Legends told as possibly true can grow in importance over time, approaching the sacred, whereas in extreme circumstances (say, religious conversions) previous myths can slowly become relegated to the realm of children's stories, only to be revived again in importance generations later.

Thus genre, like meaning, is not to be found in the stories, but rather in the outlooks of the people who tell them, both as individuals, and as members of collective social identities; identities often formed around central narratives of creation. These narrations are shared, performed, social events, and performative acts give meaning to the stories and shape their narration.

Such considerations force us at all times to acknowledge the social, performative nature of myth. This may be myth's greatest irony: while myths often promise glimpses of the transcendent, the study of myth instead leads directly back to people themselves, and their practices of myth-making.

Mythology and Culture; or, Why Are Their Myths So Strange and My Own So Sensible?

Myths are weird. Fantastical and strange, myths present bizarre narratives full of cultural-laden symbolism, difficult for the outsider to fathom. It can beggar belief to think that such strange stories could be held in reverence by otherwise reasonable-seeming people. But, and here's the important part, this is true for everyone: it's only other people's myths that seem strange. The myths of one's own culture seem sensible and understandable, and profound, of course.

In the past, this has sometimes led researchers to declare their own sacred stories as something separate from other peoples' sacred stories—"they have myths, we have a religion." Such a sentiment,

...ever indefensible academically, is understandable given the vast gulf of intercultural misunderstandings at play. First, since we have our own mythic traditions, we are encultured to approach the world in a particular way. Second, since other cultures' myths are removed from our own experiences, they may appear incomprehensible not only as narratives, but also in terms of their roles within their culture.

Myth has been popularly associated with all varieties of connotations, including fantasy, fiction, widespread error, propaganda, superstition, and more. All of these connotations are a part of the discourse, as they all reveal attitudes toward mythology, most particularly "other people's myths." The shadow side is what such connotations say about our cognitive investment in our own mythic systems, and how the worlds created in one's own myths can obfuscate understanding of other people's worlds. It's easier to believe that myths are falsehoods than to accept that truth is a culturally informed concept, variously constructed.

The nature of the sacred

What, after all, is numinous? And where is it? Does the divine rest in the heavens and the stars? The earth? The sea? Cultures with different mythic traditions will view their relationship with these elements differently. In Australian mythology, the numinous is most often located in the landscape itself, the shaping of which takes place during the Dreamtime, a transcendent reality that is, in many ways, considered to be more "real" than mundane life. The landscape, then, becomes akin to the Abrahamic concept of heaven, as well as the Bible. Just as Abrahamic followers would think it inconceivable to destroy heaven, or holy books, so Australian Aboriginal groups often look with profound dismay into developmental projects that alter the landscape itself, away from the Dreamtime and the divine. Meanwhile, Inuit myths detail the figure of Sedna, the underwater sea goddess, from whom sea life is sent forth to feed the humans. Should the rules established by her story not be followed, if the taboos are broken, then the sea life will be withheld: sea life that is the very mainstay of Inuit life and culture.

Are particular animals exalted, feared, or blamed? Abrahamic traditions are notably **anthropocentric**, as well as androcentric, wherein the creator deity appears as a male human ("God made man in his image"). The snake, at least in Christian traditions, is often identified with Satan and the embodiment of evil, while the story points out that animals and plants are mundane, not numinous, and created for the purpose of humankind. The idea of "personhood" is reserved for humans, in this tradition, a concept that may seem as natural to those within the mythic system, but less so within many other traditions. In Hinduism, the notion of reincarnation, set out in the origin myths, links all life together in a recursive hierarchy of soulfulness. Although not a religious requirement, it is perhaps easy to see why so many followers of Hinduism and other Vedic religions are avowed vegetarians. For the Chinook tribe of the Northwest Coast of North America, the salmon are mythic relatives, engaged in a symbiotic exchange of life power, which reflects the traditional importance of the salmon as the major foodstuff and source of life for the people. Among the Beng of West Africa, it is the dog that has a particularly ambivalent relationship to humans in their mythology, siding with humans against the other animals, yet also failing to properly deliver the knowledge of how to achieve immortality. Dogs are why we live, but also why we die. For the Beng, there are special rules for interacting with dogs, rules which apply to no other species. If one wants to understand why Beng treat the dogs in the way that they do, there is perhaps no better key than the myths themselves (see Gottlieb 1986). Among the Chambri of the Sepik River in Papua New Guinea, crocodiles are held to be **totemic** ancestors of people, and scarification rites of men coming of age are held to bring them closer to the crocodiles, through the imagery suggested by the scarification; while among the Ainu, the bear is the totemic ancestor, and to be hairy like a bear is considered a mark of beauty. In former times, women would often tattoo themselves with symbolic representations of a long mustache, marking beauty by indicating closeness to the divine.

Likewise, it is always an interesting exercise in mythology to get a sense for what epochs or epochal events are considered most sacred, most important, and most revered in different societies, as this gives some indication of what is considered most fundamental to particular societies. Likewise, what parts of the cosmos are highlighted—The stars? The landscape? The ocean? Not surprisingly, these emphases usually correlate with what is most important to the society that highlights them. Is it a society of pastoral herders? Settled farmers? Fishermen? These sorts of issues will all be reflected in the mythology, giving rise to some of the most interesting, compelling, and poignant variations in human cultures around the world.

Knowing the other

These brief and basic examples serve to illustrate a main theme in this book and the accompanying series: myths become explicable only through locating them in their cultural context. Therefore, to understand myth is to understand cultural relativity—the ways in which culture shapes perceptions of the world of each of us. Different cultures have vastly different cognitive worlds, and this precludes easy understanding of cultural traditions, including myths. This is not to imply that understanding others is impossible, merely that it is difficult. Of course, one might argue that one could never *really* know, from the insider's point of view, how someone in another culture thinks or processes the world—the point made early on by some anthropologists working in a postmodern perspectives (e.g., Rosaldo 1987). This may be somewhat true (depending on what is meant by "really" know), but the logic, taken to its extreme, presents a scene of solipsism: similarly, one could argue that no one could ever "really" know what it is like from any other person's perspective—even a spouse, a close family member, or an identical twin. Solipsism provides less a way forward than a helpful reminder of the difficulties of establishing socially shared knowledge of privately held experiences. To understand the other is neither fully possible nor fully impossible, but it can be made easier by understanding the varied cultural contexts in which we all operate.

Therefore, in our view, the study of mythology profits from engaging with other scholarly studies of human culture, perhaps particularly anthropology, the discipline most concerned with understanding various and highly varied cultural forms. Mythology makes particular strong appearances in the anthropological subfield of cultural anthropology, but also in the subfields of linguistic anthropology, and even archaeology.

Myths are best explored in tandem with understanding the various facets of the cultural contexts in which they are performed. The reverse way of saying this is that myths, by themselves, offer little to the analyst: they appear simply as strange tales, full of the fantastic and bizarre, inexplicable, and unknowable, and capable of creating more confusion than understanding. But when myths are investigated together with the culture in which they thrive, both the myths and the cultures become much more intelligible. For example, if we understand the importance of matrilineages in a matrilineal society, then an emphasis on a mother goddess, such as the widespread Native American Grandmother Spider deity, begins to make sense. Inversely, patrilineal societies may often invoke father gods in their mythic traditions, establishing cosmological belonging through the same scheme that provides social belonging. The anthropologist Claude Lévi-Strauss's important ideas on cognitive binaries in myth were formulated from his fieldwork in Amazonian societies with moiety systems, where the societies themselves were built on binary memberships. Although these are quite basic examples, they serve to show the importance of anthropological understandings of human cultural variation in understanding the mythologies of diverse peoples.

Like culture writ large, myth is highly variable. Since myth serves as a core narrative for meaning construction in societies, myth also provides keys toward understanding the varieties of culture. Mythological and anthropological understandings thus can work together in helping to attain wider understanding of both mythology and culture. A central myth that features a mother goddess is unlikely to appear in a patrilineal society; a myth that states that all humans are supposed to farm is unlikely to emerge in a culture of hunter-gatherers; a myth that locates the numinous in the depths of the ocean is unlikely to be found among desert nomads. These, along with many more subtle aspects, help direct the student of mythology toward understanding the cultures that tell them.

However, a word of caution, here: myths are often not straightforward charters of how to live: very often the gods act in ways antithetical to the rules of human societies. In many Native American myths, for example, Coyote engages in antisocial behaviors such as having sex with relatives, stealing, and all sorts of mischief. Sometimes his behavior shows the worst aspects of human nature, especially greed and lust, while he also creates light, brings fire to humans, and in many ways acts as a creator deity. Many of his stories can be taken as rather pedagogical examples of what *not* to do. Similarly, the Abrahamic Flood Myth does not promote mass genocide, but almost more the opposite: a message that sinfulness brings destruction. Gods and deities often act in ways antithetical to social rules, taboos, and regulations: very often the myths may detail the very formation of such social rules and regulations in the actions of deities. So the study of the relations of myth and culture cannot happen merely by examining the text of the myth itself and extrapolating elements to the culture, but must instead progress hand in hand with the study of culture, in order to better understand both myth and culture as well as the relationship between them (this point is further detailed in chapter 3, regarding the twentieth-century confluence of the anthropological and psychological schools). Nor is this solely an academic point: all cultures have their own hermeneutical traditions, ways in which the sacred stories are held to be best interpreted and applied to daily life. Such traditions provide linkages between the sacred narratives and the everyday lives of the people, traditions that need to be understood in order to best understand the myths themselves.

Mythic influences

Due to the compelling rhetorical power of mythologies, their effects can be studied from a number of disciplinary and topical outlooks: environmentalism, art, literature, music, gender, just to name a few. Mythic influences can be seen in all sorts of cultural outlooks and traditions, often pervading general discourse to such a degree that what is really myth-based can unconsciously come to be seen as "natural." For example, in Abrahamic mythology, the divine is located "in the heavens," a word meaning both the cosmos, and, more generally, "up." The deity, angels, and the afterlife of the righteous is located "up in the heavens." Not surprisingly, we see in general usage a cultural symbolic link between "up" and "good." If one gets a high grade in an American university, it means a "good" grade. If one is "feeling down," one is unhappy. If one is "rising up in a career," then one's career position is improving. Medieval cathedrals place their stained glass up high, encouraging the worshiper to gaze upwards, and to feel the beauty of heavenly ascent. Meanwhile, there are many mythic traditions that locate the numinous not in the heavens, but rather deep within the earth itself. Such a mythic tradition implies a different relation with directions: for example, in the Pueblo groups, the role of the **emergence myth**, wherein people emerged from the depths, is echoed in the central role of the underground kiva (central ritual underground structure), whose very architecture reiterates the symbolic power of the deep earth. Why is "up" good and "down" bad? These are, of course, metaphors, but they are extremely important metaphors. Metaphors are cultural constructions, and often can be viewed by investigating the symbolism of the culture's myths, the stories of how the world came to be, and the very nature of the divine. These shape the way we interact with the world surrounding us.

Increasing our understanding of the rhetorical power of myth in shaping daily lives, then, is also a way to increase intercultural understanding, and avoid harmful misunderstandings. Consider, for example, that the Hopis have a special place of reverence for the snake, an animal that traverses their mythic journey from underground to aboveground daily. When non–Native American Christians saw the Hopi religious dances incorporating the snake, the images were interpreted in a completely opposite manner: snakes are representative of evil in the Garden of Eden myth, and the impression was, therefore, that the Hopis must be satanic, and worshipping evil: a profound case of mythic misunderstanding that helped fuel various forms of religious, political, legal, and cultural persecution of Native Americans.

Why study myths from around the world?

The foregoing considerations also reveal why the study of myth must include a wide-ranging variety of mythic and cultural systems. Using the analogy of language, one can learn only so much about the human linguistic potential by studying one's own language or closely related languages. Similarly, there is a danger in studying only the "myths close to home," while attempting to understand myths generally.

Consider the case of the special place of privilege commonly given to Greco-Roman mythology in Western society, at times employed as a sort of template for understanding all mythology. This presentation has a long-standing history in European culture, and it is not going too far to say that there are mythic elements at work, here, wherein ancient Greece as the "birthplace of civilization" takes on sacred significance. Greek and Roman mythology serve as a sort of origin story for European culture and belief systems. The formation of this ideology has a long and resplendent history, from the influence of the classical philosophers on early Christian thought (for example, the profound influence of Plato's *eidos* and *logos* on early Church writings on Heaven), to the Renaissance (a word indicating a rebirth of much of the Classical world). For much of Europe's history, thinkers looked back to the Classical realm of Rome and Greece for foundational narratives. In the Renaissance, and well after, much of the foreign literature to which Europeans were exposed were Classical writers, and imagery from Classical mythology became re-ingrained in Europe's self-identity, in language, architecture, fiction, painting, and more. Although these would have been "pagan" myths, they were embraced (not without ambivalence) by the Church as appropriate cultural inspirations, much in the way that early philosophers were reworked into Christian theology.

Thus, we can observe that there are several dangers in focusing mythological researches solely, or even primarily, on the Classical realm. First, such a focus can easily veer towards myth-making rather than myth analysis. Second, many of the documented accounts were written long after the myths were living systems, and hence our data set pales in comparison with that available for many other traditions, especially contemporary ones. The data set for verifiable classical mythology as it was actually practiced is meager, in marked contrast to the large realm of secondhand data typically utilized in its representation. Third, a purely Classical focus can obscure the vast differences in human mythology: many elements in Classical mythology are "close to home" for those raised surrounded by Abrahamic traditions. Although there is no Garden of Eden story, no Noah and the Flood story in Classical traditions, one can still observe that the primary deities are anthropomorphic, androcentric (Father God), and heaven-based. Not only this, but the florescence of Christian thought in the Greco-Roman world allowed many ideas and metaphors at home in that world to be worked into Christian theology.

The preeminence given to classical Western cultures and traditions has no doubt contributed to social-evolutionist ideologies, which thought of the andro- and anthropocentric polytheism of

Classical Greece and Rome as a "step forward" from earlier beliefs, and only a "step away" from the high plateau of monotheism. The common "evolutionary" scheme of animism → polytheism → monotheism is linked with ideas of cultural supremacy, and lodged in mythic views of Greece as the "birthplace" of civilization. While understandable, this is not a helpful model in attempting to grasp the wide variety of mythic traditions.

To understand mythology, as to understand language, means to study those systems often most unlike one's own, in order to grasp the true breadth of the human potential. While Greek and Roman myths are fascinating (not only in and of themselves, but also in the way that they have continued to influence Western culture), it would be a grave mistake to stop our investigations there.

To build our knowledge of mythology, then, we must cast our net as widely as possible, with examples and investigations from throughout the world. The richest data usually come from contemporary cultures, where ethnographers can give detailed accounts not only of the performance of myths, but also the entire cultural context in which they thrive. Having said that, there are also many long-ago traditions that are well documented in literary and/or archaeological studies, and these, too, can give insights as to the vast range of potential of human mythologies.

Our work attempts to engage with myth on its own terms, by keeping faithful to a definition of myths as narratives with profound symbolic importance. "How things began" often shapes everything that follows after. The symbolic systems offered by myths become a part of our language, our worldview, our society, and our lived everyday lives.

Chapter 2

Highlights in the History of Mythological Research

The history of mythological research is a long-standing, and at times complex, story, with a list of many prominent thinkers stretching over thousands of years. This chapter will cover what we regard as the main influences in the narrative threads of the story of mythological research. We can summarize the approaches in terms of the various epochs involved. Our story begins with the pre-Christian Greek philosophical traditions, which provided many of the terms and approaches still used today in discussing mythology. This epoch is followed by that of the premodern Christian Europe. Although for much of the reign of Christianity there was comparatively little investigation of mythology, this began to change with the Renaissance, the "rebirth" of interest in Classical Greek and Roman culture, and, with this, the building interest in Classical mythologies. The Reformation challenged the Church's hegemony on philosophical discourse, allowing for a variety of newer opinions to open up the topic of myth, and the emergence of academic disciplines. Gradually, by the mid-1800s there arose three main camps of mythic researchers in Europe: the Classicists, the folklorists, and the anthropologists. The confluence of inquiries set the stage for lively debates and a proliferation of theories regarding the role of mythology. Later, psychology, and the compelling interest in the mind, was added to this mix. Researchers began to investigate the interconnections between the individual and society, via such connections as language, and the social implications of cultural performances. Increasingly, mythic research is being informed by ongoing ethnographic research, which continues to provide fresh ethnographic data with which to test classical theories, and to develop new approaches as well.

Early Greek Myths and Philosophers (Xenophanes, Democritus, Plato): An Origin Story

"Myth" is a word used to categorize certain narratives, as well as to consider them. Some form of this word was commonly employed, and discussed, throughout the entirety of European history: ancient Greece, Rome, the Holy Roman Empire, Christendom and the Middle Ages, the Renaissance, the Enlightenment, the Modern, and the Postmodern have all, in different ways, wrestled with this word and topic. To understand the term, then, requires a holistic view of how the term has been employed over time, both in regard to what the term was used to symbolize (the narratives themselves) as well as what was connoted by the term through various associations.

The English word "myth" can be derived from the Greek "*muthos*," a word that looks smartly similar to ours not only in form but in meaning. *Muthoi* (plural of *muthos*) were the tales of the gods and miraculous happenings, core narratives that gave form and function to contemporary lives. Gregory Nagy (2002) connects the usage of the Archaic Greek period distinctly with the root *mnê*, to narrate from memory. Myths were to be narrated from memory, as a means of approaching "truth" (*alêthia*) (Nagy 2002, 242).

Yet the Greek world expanded and changed beyond recognition in just a few centuries, and these changes were reflected in the changing views of myth. The city-states ceased most of their internecine warfare, and trade with foreign nations, including the ancient civilizations of Egypt and Persia, blossomed. Goods, knowledge, and stories from a vast world suffused the emerging civilization. The shift from essentially local-based culture toward a more cosmopolitan culture included the various areas of the Greek homeland, but also, and importantly, areas further and further abroad. The shift is also echoed in ideas of what myths were and what they meant. The mythologies of the ancient Greek realm were divergent, disparate, and highly dependent on locality. The emerging philosophical reflections helped displace the fundamentally local form of myths in the ancient realm, and increasingly envision the more universalist pantheon of gods and story cycles, which for many later citizens represented "true" Greek mythology.

Many of these changes emanated from Ionia, a region on the outskirts of the Greek world on the Anatolian coast. As early as the sixth century BCE, a revolution in traditional thinking about nature, its properties, and its relation to mythology began to challenge the long-dominant mythologies. Early attempts to bring these heretical ideas to the Greek mainland were routinely challenged (Anaxagoras, c. 510–428, was exiled from Athens due to a charge of impiety), but the emergence of the Ionian School, as the new philosophy was known, was to lay the groundwork for much of later Classical Greek civilization. The ancient realm of the Greek gods would never be the same. By the fifth or fourth centuries BCE, "the meaning of the ancient Greek word *muthos* was already destabilized" (Nagy 2002, 242).

As Xenophanes (c. 570–c. 475 BCE) wrote:

> The Ethiopians say that their gods are snub-nosed and black, the Thracians that theirs have light blue eyes and red hair. But if cattle and horses or lions had hands . . . horses would draw the forms of the gods like horses, and cattle like cattle, and they would make their bodies such as they each had themselves. (in Kirk et al. 1983, 169)

Later writers added to such views. Democritus (c. 460–c. 370 BCE) claimed that myths were fundamentally falsehoods, and a tool for those in power. Palaephatus' *On Unbelievable Tales* (probably dating from the late fourth century BCE) is a whole treatise of rationalistic denunciations of the local Greek mythology.

Rationality and science were emerging in Greek society. Knowledge of many aspects of science, including mathematics and physics, could be learned and passed from civilization to civilization. New discoveries could be made, and new theories developed. This heralded a florescence of scientific thinking and debate in the Classical Greek world, encapsulated by the word *logos*.

But if the laws of science were universal, then how could the myths be so particular? One answer came from the Sophists of the Greek enlightenment. The answer, for the Sophists, lay in viewing myths as cultural allegories rather than transcendent truths; allegories that, while different in form, pointed toward the same transcendent truths of science and rationality. Myths were therefore held to be in harmony with science and *logos*, if perhaps only in a poetic sort of way. By describing myths as fundamentally allegorical in nature, this movement sought to integrate the growing calls for rational thought and science with their long-standing, deeply rooted stories. Such a move sought to integrate these two divergent discourses—*muthos* and *logos*—in charting new ways for society, while at the same time allowing for foreign mythologies to be integrated into the burgeoning Greek worldview.

Plato (427–347 BCE), however, disagreed with even this acceptance of myths, and he went to great pains to emphasize a diametric opposition between *muthos* and *logos,* between myths and truths. Rather than seeing myth as serving the function of truth, it now was recast as the enemy of truth. Plato's views of myth echoes to this day: the common-day usage of "myths" as "widely held falsehoods" reiterates this dichotomy between myth and truth.

Yet, even Plato admitted a certain utility to myths, even to his own arguments for a just society. He not only transformed old myths into new ones (for example, refashioning the old myth of Eros into a new, cosmogonic one), but also created new myths, such as the myth of Er, which he created as a fundamental propagandist backdrop to his proposed utopian society, his *Republic*.

Regardless of their own changing attitudes, later Europeans often looked back to the Greek world for help in understanding mythology. As Wendy Doniger O'Flaherty (1988) states:

> It is, I think, an irony that our word for myth in most European languages, together with our basic attitude to myths, comes from ancient Greece, one of the very few cultures in the world from which we have almost no example of real, live myths, of myths as a part of a vital tradition; by the time most of the Greek myths reach us, they have been so thoroughly reworked in artistic and philosophical forms that they are mythological zombies, the walking dead. (25–26)

The Greek world that has come down to us through writings was already far removed from its ancestral mythologies, but at the same time that world was very interested in those myths, both as retellings and as a subject of discussion. Just as ancient Greek philosophy plays a large role in later European scholarly discourse, ancient Greek inquiries into mythology set the stage for a great deal of later terminology, approaches, thoughts, and ideas. This is all to say, the most important gift the ancient Greeks gave us is perhaps not their mythologies (resplendent as they may be), but perhaps their discussions *regarding* mythology.

The Christian Era: *Logos* versus *Muthos*

Both the Greek myths and Greek views of myths have continued to be an important part of later European culture. For over 1,500 years, the Christian Church controlled and influenced the ideas regarding myth. The church view held to the basic division of its own sacred origin story (the Word of God as *logos*) as true, and all others (Plato's *muthos* or myth) as error. Through this outlook, the ideas of non-Abrahamic myths were usually viewed in a particular mythic light: other traditions would be classified under "heathen idolatry," fundamentally false, **degenerative**, and, at times, pure evil. Since all people were descended from Noah, all people had been aware of God and his commands, and therefore any divergences from this mythic tradition were taken to demonstrate that such a people had degenerated away from a state of grace and moved toward evil.

Nonetheless, elements of both pre-Christian mythology and of the theoretical discourse about mythology survived in the Middle Ages. Classical scholar Luc Brisson (2004, chapter 8) summarizes several strands through which this occurred. Ancient cults persisted, especially in rural areas. Christian apologists sometimes attempted to superimpose Christian formulations on pagan, incorporating pagan shrines into Christian ones, and similarly for heroes—so that, for example, Saint Christopher became an heir to Mercury. Also, some early Christians were schooled in schools of the Greco-Roman style. Finally, now toward Christian ends, myth-interpreters continued to apply to Greek and Roman mythology some of the same theories of myth-interpretation that Greek and Roman thinkers had applied to the same myths. Prominent among these was the theory of fourth century BCE Greek Euhemerus, who argued that myths developed through the deification of real humans and events that had benefited life in earlier times (contemporary mythologists continue to refer to this principle of myth-interpretation as **euhemerism**). Brisson comments (2004, 129) that this strategy was "a two-edged sword, because, while lowering gods to the level of mortals, it confirmed their existence and enabled them to enter into history." Finally, like the Classical predecessors, some Christian myth-interpreters continued to read the pagan myths as allegories—either allegories of the physical cosmos (pagan gods becoming associated with planets and stars) or moral allegories in which various mythological characters symbolized different moral virtues and vices.

Such strategies were largely defensively motivated. In the same way that the archaic Greek period was assured of its myths' own validity, the Christian world was now assured of the validity of its own sacred origin stories, while likewise assured of the central error in other sacred origin stories. The formulation of truth versus error leads to few investigative ways forward, and, especially compared with the robust debates fomented by myth in Classical Greece, the discourse on myth was more one of redeployment than of innovation from the Roman period through to Protestant Reformation in the sixteenth century.

The Renaissance and Reformation: New Views on Old Myths (Vico, de Fontenelle, Toland, Voltaire)

An exception for Classical myths arose during the early Renaissance period, a time when Classical myths and motifs were being increasingly expressed in patronized art. The exception of Classical myths played an important role in Church thought, and in many ways, the interest and appreciation of the Classical world paved the way for the full emergence of the Renaissance. The Renaissance (roughly the 1300–1600s) was a rebirth of interest in pre-Christian Roman and especially Greek realms. This rebirth blossomed first on the Italian peninsula, the locale of the late great Roman Empire, whose name was still carried throughout Europe by the Church. Tracing back the accomplishments of the Romans led back to the Greeks, and the enormous influence that Classical Greece had on later Roman ideas. Building on its own illustrious past was one way that Italy remained engaged with the Classical realm. But Italy was also becoming increasingly involved in long-distance trade, bringing with it new ideas and scientific developments, and money for patronage systems for artistic and scholarly endeavors.

Throughout much of the era of Christendom, the Church was held to be the final authority on many aspects of society: authority, not just spiritual, but also scientific and political, were all centralized in the Church. The new discoveries, innovations, and cultural exchanges challenged the authoritative role of the Church. For example, relying on the *logos* of its sacred textual myths, the Church had mapped out the various peoples of the world as descended from Noah, held to be the last common progenitor of humanity. Semites were named from Noah's son Shem, the Hamites from Ham, and so forth. For this period, Europeans were routinely referred to as Japhethians, offspring of Noah's son Japheth. In 1492 a Genoese captain set foot on a new continent, full of strange new people who had never heard of Christ's teachings, nor were they in any way accounted for in the theocratic accounts of the world.

The intense exchanges between the Old World and the New World were one of the most transformative experiences for both, a pivotal beginning to a new global epoch in human history. In a few years, long-distance travel, trade, plunder, and diplomatic relations were bringing Europe in contact with vastly new lands, peoples, and ideas. As had happened in ancient Greece, Europe entered a period of pronounced and profound change, fueled by new discoveries, technologies, and contact with distant cultures. New conceptions of the world demanded new views of myth.

Of all the technological transformations shaking Europe during the 1400s, the largest and most impactful was the development of the printing press around 1450. In a few short years, printing presses sprung up all over Europe, and the printed word had entered into the popular culture in a way never seen before. Since previously most literacy and learning was controlled by the Church, it is perhaps not surprising that the first "bestsellers" were Martin Luther's pamphlets denouncing several aspects of the Church and calling for reforms. Although Martin Luther called for reforms, the effect was the Reformation, an epochal event that directly challenged the supremacy and supposed infallibility of the Church. The after-effects of the Protestant Reformation, and the continuing innovations and rapid changes in Europe, guided new inquiries and approaches to mythology.

One of the most compelling new views came from Giambattista Vico (1668–1744). Vico's magnum opus *The New Science* (1725) opened up new arguments about mythology, employing a rational investigation of the development of human society. Taking the biblical Flood myth as a starting point, Vico then reasoned that men had to once again begin in a primitive state, without culture or language. Vico noted the connections between language, culture, mythology, and society, and how these all must have developed together over time and changes. While not anti-Christian, Vico's approach allowed a more generous viewing of earlier mythological traditions than was previously the case. His championing of myths as an early form of culture assigns them a significance as building blocks of civilization, and reverses the Church's long-held view of all myths as degenerative.

Bernard Le Bovier de Fontenelle (1657–1757) propounded a rationalist and evolutionary model for mythology, in the notion that myths were "survivals" of earlier primitive times, a glimpse of which could still be obtained by studying contemporary "savages." "Fables" (as he termed them) were "primitive science," an idea that was echoed by many later mythologists. He did not oppose Christianity with mythology, but rather included them together, as his rationalist critiques of the Church made clear.

Anti-church figures like John Toland (1670–1722) and Voltaire (1694–1778) continued the Church's rejection of myths, while including with them those found in the Bible. Voltaire embodied much of the religious attitude of his age, which was of the Deist variety: although the existence of God was not denied, most of the sacred stories of the Bible were dismissed as mistaken superstitions— "myths" like any other.

In England, William Stukeley (1687–1765), an Anglican minister and friend of Isaac Newton, had a unique and somewhat novel approach. Fascinated by Druids, and by the Megalithic sites he associated with them, he developed a line of thought that argued that the Druids were intellectual and spiritual descendants of the early Hebrew "patriarchs," and hence, an eminently valuable subject for study. Stukeley helped ignite a popularization of study of the past religious practices in Western Europe. Stukeley's combination of fieldwork on archaeological monuments such as Avebury and Stonehenge, combined with interest in past mythologies and societies, helped consolidate what became known as "popular antiquities": a pre-disciplinary forerunner of both archaeology and folklore. The national past was becoming increasingly relevant.

Myths of the Nation: Romantic Nationalism (Herder)

The celebration of myths as establishing a national past was firmly endorsed by the works of Johann Gottfried von Herder (1744–1803), often remembered as the "Father of Nationalism." Herder was an intellectual descendent of Vico, eerily born in the year of Vico's death. Herder advocated for a search for "tribal" origins of the various "nations" now being envisioned as distinct peoples. Herder celebrated the mythology of all peoples, and throughout the world felt that the study of mythology would reveal the underlying ethnic identity, the *Volk*, of each group.

Such an idea was perhaps the first mythic challenge to the Church, and had political implications as well. After all, without a divine right enshrined by Papal Authority, where does political legitimacy lie? Political legitimacy was held to derive from God, with the Pope as the earth-bound deliverer of God's will. With the Reformation, however, much of Europe no longer followed the Pope. What, then, would be the foundation of political legitimacy?

Although not quite an idea of democracy, Herder's vision was a step toward the idea that political legitimacy should derive from the people being ruled. But who were these people? The answer, said Herder, following Vico, could be revealed through the study of folklore and the mythology of the various groups. This, then, was the beginning of the ideas of ethnonationalism, which reshaped the political landscape, and rekindled an interest in Northern Europe's ancient pagan mythologies and beliefs.

Herder's view suggested that the core narratives of the people would reveal the "nation," an idea that became a major foundation in the emerging Age of Nations and the nation-state model as the main political identity. The idea that a nation-state existed for a particular group (usually reflected in the name of the country) was a political revolution that continues to this day to be the main source of worldwide political legitimacy. Myth was being put in the service of nationalism, and later in the service of the nation-state itself.

The work of Herder set the foundations for much of the research on myth in the modern era, but it was not the only thread that informed the debates. Along with Herder we see the rise of the Romantic movement, often particularly fond of pre-Christian myths. This melded easily with the emerging political discourse of nationalism, producing the romantic nationalism, the growing belief in a sense of various set nations of people, existing from time immemorial.

As we have seen in our historical account of the word "myth," mythology and mythography (the study of mythology) are never truly separated from the rest of society, but rather can be viewed in terms of the social process. As per Vico's realization, societies have a holistic force comprising many diverse aspects, from technology to trade. As the society changes, so too do its views on myths: both the stories themselves, and the ways the stories are considered. The rise of the Enlightenment, and the eventual establishing of academic disciplines, bring the study of myth into the modern era, hand-in-hand with all the rest of the social changes. The "disciplinization" of academic studies helped foster the nineteenth century as a particularly productive and formative time period in terms of mythology, and the general and academic interest in mythology reached dizzying new heights.

The Nineteenth Century: Colonialism, Change, and the Emergence of Academic Disciplines

Radical changes were shaking European civilization and, with these, the view of mythology. While Deists were insisting that all myths—biblical and otherwise—were largely false, others continued to see promise in mythology in terms of the overall development of societies, both at home and abroad. While Classical myths continued to be appreciated in many circles, two other distinct branches were emerging: one was the school of "local" mythic study, represented by the folklorists, while another was the school of "foreign" mythic study, represented by the anthropologists. Both the understanding of European people's past and humanity at large were continuing to change through the Enlightenment and continuing into the modern era.

The emergence of mythology studies in the nineteenth century can be divided into three main (yet overlapping) camps: the folklorists, the anthropologists, and the Classicists. The Classicist school had the ancient pedigree: descending from the scholarly erudition of the Church, the Classicists became intent on studying mythologies, particularly from the Greco-Roman era. One essential tool was that of **philology**. Philology, or the study of changes in textual language, had long been a concern for the Church: with many sacred writings abounding in hand-copied form, which was the eldest, the most "original"? Philology held that the earliest texts were the most correct texts, as later scribes might make errors or changes in their copies. Since the Word of God was held to be true, the search for "original" texts was an important aspect of Church scholarship. The philological move had profound implications for both the anthropological and particularly the folkloric school, as it helped shape the ideas that the earliest versions were therefore better than later versions, as the quest for origins came to dominate the approach toward mythology in general. The myths of the Classical realm continued to be important touchstones for all three disciplinary approaches, although the folklorists and anthropologists focused their researches elsewhere.

The Rise of Folklore Studies: Becoming Germany (Brothers Grimm, Schwartz, Mannhardt)

In developing the folkloric approach, none were more impactful than the brothers Wilhelm Grimm (1786–1859) and Jacob Grimm (1785–1863). The Brothers Grimm were intellectual descendants of Herder, to be sure, yet unlike Herder's more universal claim that each society's myth was important, the Grimms steadfastly remained interested in bringing Herder's ideas to the study of German folklore, mythology, and identity, always with an eye toward the political implications. Inspired by the ideas of philologists for uncovering earlier, more "authentic" textual traditions, the Grimms turned their attention to German folklore. The Brothers Grimm, more than any other scholars, are remembered as the founders of modern folklore studies. Their seminal work *Kinder- und HausMärchen* (*Children's and Household Tales*), published in 1812, established the utility of folklore in establishing national identity, and was a watershed publication. In this bestseller, the Grimms had combined their interest in romantic nationalism, with philology, all in the service of uncovering the "soul" of the German people. Setting their work aside from those who saw folk tales as devices for literary productions (such as the contemporaneous Hans Christian Andersen), the Grimms held that the rougher, earlier versions were inherently "purer" than literary retellings, and hence established a scientific methodology for collecting and recording folk stories.

The formation of the discipline of folklore can be seen in many aspects of the Grimms' work. For example, while their first work was on tales, this was followed by a two-volume work on legends, *Deutsche Sagen* (*German Legends*) in 1816 and 1818, which in turn was followed by Jacob Grimm's 1835 wildly influential work on mythology, *Deutsche Mythologie* (*German Mythology*). Besides helping to establish the genre categories, the Grimms also established the basic ideas of folklore research, by paying careful, scientific attention to the data, that being the performances of the folklore. The Grimms insisted that folklore should not be edited or "improved" (an insistence that they did not always themselves follow). The career of the Grimms can scarcely be overestimated in terms of the development of the study of mythology. Melding the study of mythology with that of folklore, they turned the idea of mythology firmly away from the Classical studies, and toward an inward look at the traditions of the various European countries themselves. This also wedded early folklore research to the general ideology of romantic nationalism. Throughout Europe, many researchers were inspired by the Grimms' efforts, and the field of folklore as an independent discipline blossomed.

Other important researchers soon followed the Grimms' trail. In Germany, mythological research was carried out by figures such as F. L. W. Schwartz (1821–1899) and Wilhelm Mannhardt (1831–1880). Schwartz took a different tack toward understanding mythology. The country folk still remembered the various creatures of "lower mythology" (elves, dwarves, spirits of the forest, etc.), which, although not gods, do show up in many mythological accounts (such as Thor getting his hammer from the dwarves, etc.). Schwartz reasoned that these various spirits were the oldest mythology, and that the more "refined" great gods were introduced at later stages. For Schwartz, then, to understand the local, and ancient, was to understand the still-living traditions of the figures of lower mythology. This returned a focus and attention to the ongoing rural and agrarian beliefs of country folk, not in terms of reconstructing ancient philologies, but in understanding how these "primitive mythologies" were still active and alive. His view was given further credence by the pioneering work of Mannhardt, who relied on exhaustive surveys to take stock of the ongoing agrarian beliefs in figures of lower mythology. Mannhardt demonstrated ongoing beliefs in figures of lower mythology, which he then connected to ancient ideas of both Greeks and Teutonic tribes. Mannhardt's work is notable in its thoroughness of collecting data, the importance given to ongoing folk customs and stories, and the reconnecting of this with the realm of the Classicists, as well as the growing interest in the development of human civilization and culture.

Throughout Europe, folklore became the preeminent discipline for studying mythology, and the material was in the people themselves, the folk (*das Volk*). The political implications can easily be witnessed in terms of the countries that embraced this new study. For the most part, the areas of Europe where folklore studies particularly blossomed were those areas striving to assert a national identity. Emerging nation-states like Ireland, Estonia, Germany, and Finland led the way in new works and theories. The more established, imperial, states, such as the United Kingdom and France, were more influenced by the rapid rise of global trade and the growth of colonialism, and therefore became more invested in the anthropological school, which sought to look at mythology in a comparative manner, particularly in terms of the development of civilizations.

While folklorists could claim a fair amount of ease in recording tales, mythology proved a harder nut to crack. Since the ancient mythology was no longer extant in Europe (lower mythologies excepted) and the only written records came from Christian writers, mythology would have to be *reconstructed*, and this pushed the national folklorists to engage in varying levels of reconstruction. For the Grimms, their reconstructions of German mythology relied heavily on material from the Icelandic sagas.

Influences from India: Philology and the Search for the *Ur*-Form (Benfey)

Philology, or the general reconstruction of culture based on linguistic reconstructions, continued to be a prime avenue for the folkloric mythologists. One of the most remarkable developments was the growing realization that the priestly Sanskrit language of India was cognate with the major European languages, gradually becoming a recognition of the Indo-European language family. Folklorically, materials from India were having an effect as well. One interesting strand of thought became known as the Out of India hypothesis, which held that much of European culture had originated in India. This outlook was heralded by the warm reception of the work of Theodor Benfey (1809–1881). Benfey published a definitive edition of the *Panchatantra*, a collection of ancient Indian animal fables, that was widely read and discussed in the growing Orientalist discourse. It was evident that many of these stories were reminiscent of Aesop's Fables, and the ongoing quest for origins, for the *ur*-form of European cultures, soon led in an unexpected direction: India. The "Out of India" theory proposed that India, and the Sanskrit language was the original "home" of the "Aryan" peoples and cultures. This displacement of "homeland" from Europe to India can be seen as a natural outgrowth of the philological method combined with the idea of essential organic unity of a "people"—a fundamental belief of romantic nationalism. If there are older versions in India of a tale than in Europe, then, it was reasoned, India must have been the original "homeland" of the Europeans, usually now postulated as "Aryans," an ancient Indian group. Problematically, these notions were transmuted by some into the idea of "Aryan supremacy," which helped to ensconce attitudes of racial hierarchies, enabling the growth of scientific racism, the slave trade, and the genocide of many indigenous groups.

Myth as Archaic Poetry from the Heavens (Müller)

Other mythologists had different theoretical conclusions drawn from the still-extant mythological material in India. One of the most profoundly influential approaches was that of Max Müller. Friedrich Max Müller (1823–1900), generally known as Max Müller, was a philologist and Orientalist who had undertaken a study of Indian mythic traditions. Inspired by the emerging recognition of the historical relatedness of the Indo-European languages, Müller published well-received arguments regarding the nature of mythology, generally. Rather than utilizing the "Out of India" theory, Müller instead argued for a universalist approach to myth, building from his analysis of Sanskrit material, yet applying these to rather forceful conclusions of theories that had been suggested at various times throughout the history of mythography.

Müller's approach was, rather dogmatically, that all men began by worshipping the sun. The stories in myths, and the deities, were originally all analogies to help explain natural phenomena, such as why the sun rises, and sets, and so on. Müller's phenomenal success in propounding these rather reductive views has to be taken in light of the context of the day. Müller's approaches combined several fashionable pursuits: study of Indian mythic traditions, the romantic tradition of extolling Nature, philology, and the growing interest in the anthropological approach of human cultural development. While Müller's theories seem a bit embarrassing in hindsight, he was unquestionably the most influential mythologist of his day. Müller argued that all myths were dimly remembered allegories of natural processes, distorted through what he termed the "disease of language"—meaning that as languages changed over time, the original meanings of the myths were largely forgotten (only to be discovered later by intrepid philologists!). **Solar mythology** argued for the preeminence of the sun in all the world's mythologies, although further iterations of Müller's approach added in allegories of other natural processes, such as the moon, tides, wind, etc., giving rise to the slightly expanded name of Nature Mythologies.

Language and Indo-European Mythology (Müller, Dumézil)

Müller's interest in foreign traditions, universal explanations, and cultural evolution placed him in the growing anthropological camp of scholars, all of whom were increasingly influenced by the vast amounts of new mythological information available. But his theories on solar mythology were vigorously debated by the English folklorist school, and eventually forcefully rejected. And another aspect of Müller's work also came to be seen as increasingly problematic in the face of growing scholarly evidence concerning languages and mythologies. Specifically, with his great enthusiasm for locating interconnections between different languages and mythologies, and with only limited evidence to draw upon, Müller had often posited such connections on the slimmest basis, sometimes as little as two languages sharing a single similar-appearing syllable. As evidence accumulated, the historical connections cavalierly posited by Müller and his followers came in for increasing ridicule, to the point where linguistically based **comparative mythology**, even when restricted to Indo-European languages, was regarded with skepticism. In the mid-twentieth century, however, Indo-Europeanist Georges Dumézil spearheaded a significant revival of Indo-European comparativist study of mythology, through an approach that was seen by many as providing a tighter method for positing historical interconnections. Dumézil looked for connections in mythologies not on the level of isolated elements such as particular words or syllables, but in terms of a model of society that he regarded as common to Indo-European peoples and reflected in their languages, mythologies, and social hierarchies. The most important feature of Dumézil's proposed model was a schema of a society made up of three essential components or "functions"—ruler, warrior, agriculturalist. While critics saw even this schema as overly general, it at least moved the focus of comparison from element to "system," and it intrinsically connected the study of mythology to concerns, such as social structure, that anthropologists were coming to see as unavoidable in the study of mythology.

Who Are the British? Mythology and the Search for a Nation's Soul (Keightley, Hyde, Campbell, Rhys, Nutt)

In England, Arthurian materials, along with a general interest in the Druids and the megalithic monuments, had long been the domain of the antiquarians. The influences of the Grimms helped to separate the strands of popular antiquities into two very separate disciplines, folklore and archaeology, which have largely retained their separation ever since. Mythic research in England reveals some of its cultural tensions. England was emerging as a major colonial power, and had a growing interest in mythologies from around the world. Yet, it also had strong local and national interests—not just in England itself, but even more so in the other, more Celtic, parts of the British isles—Ireland, Wales, and Scotland, particularly.

Ireland especially was an early adopter of the Grimms' methods and theories, and the work of Thomas Keightley (1789–1872) on *The Fairy Mythology* (1828) so impressed the Grimms that they translated his work into German. The rising Celtic interest can be seen in part as a reaction against the English colonial domination, buttressed by strong traditions of native storytelling. More than anywhere else in Europe, Ireland (and to a lesser degree, Scotland) had never lost the tradition of storytelling, including many stories, customs, and traditions that were deeply enmeshed with myth. Stretching back in time, one reason may have been the rather unique status of Ireland in terms of Christian Europe: unlike all other areas, Ireland converted to Christianity as an internal, rather than external, process. Although an early adopter of Christianity, Ireland was never politically part of the Roman Empire. Many of its early saints had been former Druids, and its indigenous traditions had never been demonized in the same way that had befallen traditions elsewhere. Until the late 1800s, the Irish Church retained a high degree of autonomy from the Roman Catholic Church. The professional storytellers, or *seanachie*, were descendants of the Bardic Order, which itself was a descendent of the Druidic order. These long-standing cultural traditions, and identity, were under sustained and at times brutal colonial domination from England. In the emerging age of romantic nationalism, there could be fewer grounds more fertile for mythic research than in Ireland, and folklore became, and remains, a *cause célèbre*. Eventually, folklore studies would pave the way for Irish independence from the United Kingdom—Ireland's first president, Douglas Hyde (1860–1949), was first and foremost a folklorist—but in the nineteenth century, much of the support for research in Irish studies came from sympathetic publishers in England.

Material emerged from other parts of the Celtic realm: John Francis Campbell of Islay engaged in prodigious folklore collecting in Scotland, whereas John Rhys (1840–1916) took up the more difficult attempt of reconstructing mythologies of ancient Wales.

In England, the question of what England's "soul" was—Celtic or Teutonic—provided an impetus behind many of the ideas that were being hotly debated. Research into England's mythologies tended to focus on Arthurian materials, and arguments raged as to whether this represented Celtic or Germanic traditions. The Celtic school was championed by such figures as Alfred Nutt (1856–1910), who was active as a folklorist and Celticist, and used his publishing company to make available a great deal of writing on mythic and Celtic themes.

In general, all three traditions—Classics, folklore, and anthropology—formed a potent mix in the British Isles, with most scholars being influenced by these different schools.

Anthropology and Empire: Social Evolution and Savage Survivals (Spencer, Tylor)

With the establishment of Darwinism as the basis for biological development, many scholars turned to Spencerism, which offered an analogous theory of "social evolution," arguing that societies and cultures "evolved" like organisms. The "evolutionary" idea of mythology had been around for some time already, but here it is used with folklore and anthropology to put forth a frequent theme: myth could be envisioned as "savage survivals."

Spencerism worked well with the growing influence of Colonial belief in the inferiority of non-Europeans and their mythological traditions, and for many writers of this time, folklore was all composed of survivals of a much earlier phase of history. This can also be seen as an outgrowth of the philological approach, which held as its premise the promise of a singular, magnificent origin, progressively devalued over time.

The anthropological school was mainly concerned with understanding the vast repertoire of human mythologies, rather than reconstructing that of Europeans' own home countries. The usually cited founder of cultural anthropology is Sir Edward Burnett Tylor (1832–1917). Tylor was inspired by a trip to Mexico, where he both talked with locals and took in archaeological monuments. Influenced by Spencer, Tylor is the scholar most influential in proposing the "unilineal theory of cultural evolution": a belief that all cultures "evolved" in the same manner, if at different rates. The social evolutionists held that there had been a "stage" development, usually tripartite, with the "savages" forming the earlier, lower, and more primitive ranks. "Savages" had mythology, barbarian tribal peoples had "legends," and the "civilized" had emerged through those stages into the triumphal arrival of science. In terms of folklore, civilized people, according to this scheme, only had fairy tales. Moreover, since all societies developed through the same stages, albeit at different rates, ethnographic evidence from contemporary peoples, geographically distant from Europe and still living at the "savage" stage, could be used to help illuminate inadequately understood aspects of European history—that is, the times in which Europeans themselves were still savages or barbarians. When social evolutionists of the nineteenth century use the term "comparative method," usually they have in mind this practice of making comparisons between geographically distant peoples allegedly occupying the same evolutionary stage, and thus able to throw light on one another's customs and modes of thought. The method was widely accepted by social thinkers in the nineteenth century and gave rise to numerous variations, including Sigmund Freud's claim to have found in aboriginal Australian "totemism" a clue to the thinking of neurotic modern Europeans—neurosis, in Freud's view, amounting to regression by modern individuals to an earlier evolutionary stage.

Mythology, in E. B. Tylor's view, was a sort of "primitive science." This is an important point, since—unlike many contemporaries—Tylor held that the difference between "civilized" and "primitive" people was simply their culture, not their innate biology or mental abilities. Still, Tylor effectively denied mythology to "civilized" man, replacing it with science, and "fairy tales"—stories told as not true, and mostly good for bedtime stories for children. Folklore was increasingly viewed as survivals from a more savage stage of a society's development. In the most extreme position of this, all fairy tales were held to be originally myths. Thus, Goldilocks and the Three Bears was explained as a devolved version of early bear worship, for example.

Combining Folklore and Anthropology in the "Great Debates" in Britain (Clodd, Gomme, Lang, Frazer)

Folklorists such as Edward Clodd (1840–1930) and Sir George Laurence Gomme (1853–1916) fused their understanding of mythology with an acceptance of anthropology's evolutionary stages of human culture. As Gomme wrote:

> The great fact necessary to bear in mind is that the people of a modern culture area have an anthropological as well as a national or political history, and that it is only the anthropological history which can explain the meaning and existence of folklore. (1908, xiii)

Nonetheless, there were other writers instead attracted to the "noble savage" ideology, an ideology that had particular resonance for the Celtic areas of the British Isles. Andrew Lang (1844–1912) makes a good example of this: a Classicist, but primarily a folklorist interested in Celtic materials, Lang was attracted to the supernatural, and convinced that the popularity of such practices as ghost-hunting in contemporary England was one indication that "savages" were not so different in mentality. Where others saw primitive belief and superstition, Lang argued for strong spirituality and nobleness of spirit.

More in line with Tylor's thought was the Classicist, folklorist, and anthropologist Sir James George Frazer (1854–1941), who helped popularize researches into mythology more than anyone of his time, particularly with his ongoing series of books entitled *The Golden Bough*, a massive comparative compendium of ritual practices and mythologies from all over the world, published in numerous volumes between 1890 and 1915. Many of his examples used in his book have been since questioned, as Frazer relied on second-hand accounts from traders and missionaries, yet several ideas that Frazer proposed have continued to have relevance. His insistence on putting Abrahamic mythology in the same category of world mythology is, of course, helpful in the dispassionate study of mythology, generally. He was also a key figure in developing anthropology as a discipline, perhaps most famously by his student, Bronisław Malinowski, who helped pioneer anthropological field research, vastly improving its data set. But Frazer can also be seen in the context of an important development in the study of mythology, generally: that being the role of ritual.

A New Take on Old Classics: The Myth-Ritual School (Smith, Frazer, Harrison)

While many of the approaches championed in the nineteenth century have analogues in previous—including Classical Greek— writers, the myth-ritual approach is a relatively original outlook on myths. Frazer was an adherent, and popularizer, of this approach, but its foundations can be seen put forth by Frazer's friend, William Robertson Smith (1846–1894). Smith, an Orientalist and scholar of the Old Testament, developed an approach that examined not so much the narratives or religious beliefs, but rather the practices, the rituals themselves. According to Smith, it was the rituals that tended to remain constant, while the interpretations of those rituals, and the mythic stories derived from them, could fluctuate wildly. Myths, in this view, derived from the rituals, not vice versa.

Frazer adopted this approach in his overall view of mythology. Frazer was interested in a particular "stage" of development, the transition between the ages of magic, and the development of religion. For Frazer, this transition, from ritual to belief, was characterized by the rise of mythology. Magic, which is to say superstitious thinking, is for Frazer characterized by ritual actions, combined with belief. Like Tylor, Frazer believed that mythology thus served the functions of trying to understand and control the world as a primitive science, via the performance of ritual actions. It is a testament to Frazer's novel thinking that his two categories of "sympathetic magic," contagious and homeopathic ("like produces like"), continue to have wide application toward understanding magic rituals, and folk beliefs, today.

Another one of Frazer's students developed an even stronger theory of the link between myth and ritual, this time relying on exclusively Classical materials. Jane Harrison (1850–1928) was a remarkable figure, one of the few women able to penetrate into the male-dominated academic realm in the nineteenth century. Her novel approaches to Greek Classics included the use of archaeology alongside the Classical texts, which transformed Classics as a discipline. In moving the study of Classics to the "real world," she was also influenced by the anthropological accounts from around the world, including by her mentor, Frazer. In her examination of some of the earliest Greek works, Harrison began to argue that the origin for all the myths lay in the rituals themselves. A thespian, Harrison was interested in the origins of drama. For her, drama arose from rituals, and gradually the rituals shaped the stories. Harrison's myth-ritual theory is not only a proposed basis for the development of myth, but also for the proposed development of theater. As such, Harrison provides one of the more extreme views of the myth-ritual school: that myth in all cases derives from ritual, and from the spiritual impact that engaging in ritual has for the worshippers. Rather than seeing myth and ritual in distinct stages of development, Harrison asserts that they work together in a myth-ritual stage of culture.

The myth-ritual school has invited numerous proponents and critics who have applied the idea to a wide variety of societies and time periods. While further research has tempered some of the extreme statements of the early writers, the idea that myths are often performed in the heightened context of rituals remains valid, and many scholars continue to find efficacy in examining both together. As with many totalizing explanations, the myth-ritual approach might not suffice. Certainly the idea of unilineal stage development of culture has been abandoned by later anthropologists. Further, myths and rituals are not always found together. Yet the acknowledgment that myths are often expressed via ritual retains a good deal of utility in many cases, providing one more tool for the mythographer's toolkit.

While the British Isles shows the productive confluence of Classics, folklore, and anthropology toward the study of myth during the nineteenth century, the folklore school on the continent was continuing to develop new research methods and theories arising out of early philological orientations and emerging romantic nationalism. The search for ancient origins for a "nation" of people continued to flavor a great deal of the research, particularly in those areas striving to achieve political status as a nation-state.

Finland: Myth, Nation, and the Historic-Geographic Method (Lönnrot)

One important and long-standing tradition of scholarship emanated from Finland, in what became known as the "Finnish method" of folklore studies. During the heady days of the folklore revolution sweeping Europe, Finland lacked recognition as a nation. Politically, it was controlled by Sweden, with the Swedish language being used in educational and official contexts. It was assumed by many Swedes that this part of "eastern Sweden" would soon become fully Swedish, and Finnish, Finns, and Finland would fade from existence. For people opposing this vision, "discovering" a national corpus of folklore was the natural way forward. Elias Lönnrot (1802–1884) was a philologist and folklorist, very much in the manner of the Grimms. Lönnrot undertook fieldwork research to the more rural and remote parts of the countryside, publishing what he labeled the *Kalevala*. The impact of the *Kalevala* in terms of Finland's cultural and political history can scarcely be overstated. It is often labeled as the "national epic," with a profound and continuing influence. Yet it is important to note that the *Kalevala* was published in two very distinct versions. The earlier (1835) version was a collection of various poems from various areas. Yet the second, much grander version (1849) was a different sort of text altogether. In this text, the poems had been expanded, and arranged on a sort of lineal narrative, stretching from mythic time and the beginning of the world all the way up to the near-historic periods. This version was heavily edited and modified by Lönnrot, in essence creating what was needed: a national myth. In this example, we can see how the confluence of philology and folklore studies converged on the "dis-covering" of a grand, unified, mythic past—albeit with the extended efforts of the folklorist/author, Lönnrot. Likewise, and likewise reminiscent of the Grimms, Lönnrot also compiled the first Finnish-Swedish dictionary, although many of his Finnish terms were either "reconstructed" by Lönnrot himself, or complete neologisms that he coined for the project. Regardless, this, too, worked: many of his new words found their way into the reinvigorated Finnish language. In Lönnrot's efforts, we can see a sort of self-fulfilling prophecy enacted by reconstructionist work, alongside a dedicated political expediency. This also once again highlights the dangers in mythography: in presenting mythic materials, is one merely reflecting the myths of the people, or is one actively engaged in *creating* new myths?

From Folk to Lore: The Historic-Geographic Method (the Krohns, von Sydow, Aarne)

The popularity of the *Kalevala* spurred on both folklore and political activism in Finland. Julius Krohn (1835–1888) was an early agitator for Finnish independence, but he is now widely remembered for his careful, insightful work on how best to extend the philological enterprise into folklore studies. Krohn developed what is now known as the "**historic-geographic method.**" This method involves careful comparisons of differing versions of folklore, alongside a geographic and historical awareness, in order to trace the history of any specific item of folklore. His work was carried on after his death by his son, Kaarle Krohn (1863–1933), who championed the method. As a result, the method became known variously as the "Finnish method," or the "Krohn method," as well as the now-accepted "historic-geographic method."

Although stemming from the already-existing philological traditions of romantic nationalism, the historic-geographic method led research into some new and interesting directions. If one could rely on data to provide information as to where a piece of folklore came from, and how it changed over time, this opened up whole new realms of inquiry. Rather than being restricted to the development of a specific cultural group, a nation, now folklore studies could focus instead on the material itself: not the folk, but the lore. As the folkloric investigations continued apace throughout much of Europe, it soon became clear that, rather than being developed by "a people" and kept within a group, folklore was instead frequently widely distributed and shared. Which is all to say, the initial folklore project which sought to "find" Herder's spirit of a nation through careful folklore research was now leading in the opposite direction. The data coming in suggested, instead, that much of folklore was diffused over various linguistic and ethnic groups. Further, with careful attention to detail, it might be possible to trace when and where this occurred, as well as noting the changes that each group might make. The concept of folklore as evidence of cultural evolution was now giving way to data suggesting instead widespread diffusion, and adaptation. Swedish folklorist Carl Wilhelm von Sydow (1878–1952) provided the term "oicotype" to refer to the adaptation of folklore of a particular group, and argued that diffusion required no mass migrations of people, and therefore no "original" people, since folklore spread easily enough from person to person.

One more Finn, a student of Kaarle Krohn, needs mentioning. Antti Aarne (1867–1925), inspired by Kaarle Krohn's work on folk tales and his theories of diffusion, set out to create a classification system of tales, for general scholarly comparison in multiple countries. This project already shows the sea change of attitude toward material in the folklore scholarship: expanding away from the national and evolutionary, folklore scholarship was now increasingly international and focused on diffusion. Although a work on tales, rather than myths, Aarne's work helped shift the focus in folklore scholarship broadly, and helped the "Finnish school" become widely known and emulated worldwide. When Aarne died before completing his task, the American Stith Thompson (1885–1976) was brought in to complete it. The Aarne-Thompson tale type index became a standard of the discipline, and various other tale type indexes have tried to accomplish much of the same in many other parts of the world.

Throughout the development of folklore as a discipline, its ties to the quest for national origins produced a great number of philological reconstructive attempts, the results of which can be easily critiqued by today's standards. At the same time, the essentially national and local characteristic of folklore studies existed alongside the internationalization of the discipline, which required international connections to the world of scholarship. This relationship produced new and important methodologies still used today, such as the role of fieldwork, folklore collecting, and the development of folklore archives. As the historic-geographic method became refined and tested against the growing data set in numerous archives, the discipline began to challenge its ethnic essentialist assumptions, and began to understand the wide role of diffusion. Folklore, it was increasingly thought, was passed on and spread by performances. Gradually the role of performance, and the role of the people, began to rise in importance in the study of mythology. Stories could travel, even without large-scale movements of people. The role of diffusion played against the anthropologist's preference for evolutionary roles of mythology, and against the very notion of stories representing "stages" of cultural development.

Twentieth-Century Studies: Ethnography, Anthropology, Sociology

As the study of mythology entered the twentieth century, both disciplines of folklore and anthropology were maturing, as more and better data became increasingly available. This was especially true for anthropology, which continued to encounter radically different mythic views around the world. In the Americas, the rise of anthropology was a meeting ground of European thought and New World peoples and myths. Early anthropological investigations remained mired in racist views of biological cultural determinism and strict ideas of "stages" of social evolutionary development. Such viewpoints can be seen within the context of the politics of the time, allowing a moral cover for genocide, slavery, and wars of conquest that had, over a 400-year history, wrested dominion of the New World from its indigenous owners to its new, European, claimants. By the turn of the twentieth century, this process was largely complete. At about this time, new views and applications of the American school of both anthropology and folklore came from outside of America, in part, oddly enough, because of the continuing legacy of Sir James George Frazer.

American Anthropology: From Hierarchies to Cultural Relativity (Boas)

Franz Boas (1858–1942) became interested in mythology through Frazer's writings, but his real introduction to anthropology came when he spent long periods of winter with Inuit groups on Baffin Island. During this intensive research period, he became impressed with the ability and culture of the Inuit. Far from being "savages," he found them to be admirable, intelligent, and extremely capable. After his time with them, he began research with groups of Native Americans in the Pacific Northwest. Boas was able to successfully challenge both the race-based biocultural arguments of the day, as well as the belief in stage developments. These were important victories, as they turned the attention of anthropologists toward the role of culture as created via social learning as the central analytical concept of anthropology.

Boas is known as the "father of American Anthropology" for these ideological developments, as well as his contributions to building American anthropology into a university discipline. He helped found the *Journal of American Anthropology* in 1899, and the American Anthropological Association in 1902. His students included luminaries such as Ruth Benedict, Margaret Mead, Melville J. Herskovitz, Alfred Kroeber, Robert Lowie, Edward Sapir, Elsie Clews Parsons, Paul Radin, Ashley Montagu, Frederica de Laguna, and Zora Neale Hurston, among many others. Further, he helped set the standard for anthropological work, including participant observation (where one participates as fully as possible with the group in question, while continuing to critically observe), empiricism, and cultural relativism. Boas also brought with him an interest in folklore, and argued forcefully that folklore should be considered a part of anthropology. In 1908 he became editor of the *Journal of American Folklore*, and he regularly published on mythological themes. For Boas, and his students and intellectual descendants, folklore and mythology was not something to be reconstructed using philology; rather, it was to be experienced, appreciated, collected, and recorded from living groups, all with a careful eye toward the performances and contexts. Such data was vastly more rich than the troubled fragments used in Europe; it also spelled a growing separation of folklore studies between Europe and America. Europe increasingly defined the discipline of folklore in terms of rural peasants (*das Volk*), while American folklore moved away from both literary and reconstructive foci, and increasingly moved toward contemporary data from any and all groups. In short, Boas was just the sort of outsider that America needed to reorient culture and mythology studies away from reconstructions, and toward descriptions; away from evolution, and increasingly toward diffusion; away from racism, and increasingly toward cultural relativism.

Anthropology as Ethnography (Malinowski)

Nor was Boas alone in this project. One of Frazer's students, Bronisław Malinowski (1884–1942), undertook similarly long extended fieldwork in the Trobriand Islands in Melanesia. This experience provided him with a firm belief in the importance of fieldwork and participant observation—a notable break from his mentor's problematic use of at-times suspect ethnographic accounts. Malinowski was able to witness not just a textual representation of myth, but also how myths played out over the course of years in communities. For Malinowski, the importance of myth was not in the story, nor the ritual, so much as it was in the role that the mythology played in organizing the social world. This led to Malinowski's major contribution to the perspective of **functionalism**: the study of how cultural elements, including mythology, function within a society to serve basic human needs, including psychological needs.

Malinowksi was a flamboyant writer who set out his views on the new way to study myth in memorable and colorful polemics. Perhaps most thought-provoking is the relationship he implies between how we study myth and what we think myth *is*. Malinowski juxtaposed the anthropologist living in the middle of a village and listening to people actually narrate stories about the origin of their clans and about perilous voyages beyond the atoll—while seeing and hearing all of this in operation—to that of nineteenth-century **armchair** solar-mythologists sitting in their comfortable studies loftily imagining that mythology arose from archaic enrapturement with the heavens. No, insists Malinowski, myth arises not as an "idle rhapsody" (1992, 196) but as a "hard-working, extremely important social force" rooted in the needs, challenges, and treacheries of real life. In one of the most often-quoted passages of myth-study, Malinowski proclaims:

> Myth fulfils in primitive culture an indispensable function: it expresses, enhances, and codifies belief; it safeguards and enforces morality; it vouches for the efficiency of ritual and contains practical rules for the guidance of man. Myth is thus a vital ingredient of human civilization: it is not an idle tale but a hard-worked active force; it is not an intellectual explanation or an artistic imagery, but a pragmatic charter of primitive faith and moral wisdom. (1992, 199)

Although Boas and others also deserve credit, it was Malinowski more than any other researcher who created the "myth" of the modern anthropologist, and who made intensive and immersive experience with a culture a precondition for understanding its mythology, a hallmark of anthropological research that remains today. Why study myth from crusty old library books, asks Malinowski, when the field researcher has "the myth-maker at his elbow" (1992, 198)? Besides recording the text itself, the researcher studying myth in its social context "has a host of authentic commentators to draw upon; still more he has the fullness of life itself from which the myth has been born" (1992, 198). Tellingly, while his sojourn in the Trobriand Islands allowed him to experience the living reality of myth in a way that his armchair predecessors could not, Malinowski still managed to only partially move beyond their preconception that myth is something essentially "primitive." Although in Malinowski's writings one finds numerous comments that analogize social life in the Trobriands to that in modern Europe, he still relied more heavily on the term "myth" for the former than for the latter. The tension can be seen even in the passage quoted above; at one point, myth is "thus a vital ingredient of human civilization"—presumably he means all human civilization—but at two other points it is linked specifically with the "primitive" ("primitive culture," "primitive faith and moral wisdom").

Whatever their other benefits and defects, Malinowski's polemics powerfully dramatized the significant divide between two approaches to myth study, one based on literary-historical textual analysis, the other on participatory field research. If Malinowski was ready to pronounce the former tradition passé, the longer historical judgment has been more balanced, with both traditions finding much to learn from the other. In cases in which they have only bare texts to work with, literary-historical scholars can take inspiration about possible social functions of myth from the findings of field researchers, and some indeed have attempted to draw on ethnographic analogies in such cases. On the basis of a field project of a limited temporal duration, a field researcher might imagine that the social situation he or she confronts may be entirely static, but the many processes of historical change through time in mythologies that have been demonstrated through careful literary-historical analysis can at the least provide a useful caution to the field research ready to conclude that the researcher has discovered a "timeless" society or mythology.

Mythic Thought as Community (Durkheim, Lévy-Bruhl)

Born the same year as Boas, Émile Durkheim (1858–1917) was also interested in the role of myth for the human community. Durkheim was one of the major founders of twentieth-century sociology, and his ideas of the social bonding of communities, organized around religion, proved to have an enduring impact. Durkheim perceived the difference between "primitive" communities and "modern" ones as largely a matter of size: communities not linked in day-to-day interactions had to have collective beliefs and sentiments held in common, and these, for him, were the essential functions of religions. Durkheim was critiqued by the folklorist Arnold van Gennep (1873–1957) as lacking quality field data, and building his theories of the role of ritual and religion on untrustworthy sources. Nonetheless, Durkheim's ideas of culture as an arena of communal participation proved influential to many scholars. One of these was Lucien Lévy-Bruhl (1857–1939), who was interested in ideas of the "primitive mind." Lévy-Bruhl saw a qualitative difference between "primitive" and "modern" thought, in that while the latter used reflection and logic, the former used "mystical participation" in the realm of ritual, mythology, and superstition. Ultimately, though, he abandoned the strong primitive/modern dichotomy, concluding that both modes of thought were to be found in all peoples.

The Rise of Psychology (Descartes, Locke, Wundt)

As can be seen, the interest in "the mind" was growing in importance in mythic studies: what was the relationship between thought and myth?

Throughout the growth of the Enlightenment, the individual had been rising in importance. René Descartes (1596–1650) had opened up these discussions early on in his formulation of rationalism: *cogito, ergo sum* ("I think, therefore I am"), paving the way for investigation of the mind, which he also called the soul. A devout Catholic, Descartes believed that all knowledge was derived from God, via religion. This aspect of his theories was critiqued by John Locke (1632–1704), who argued instead that all knowledge was acquired through experience.

A modification to Locke's empiricism was proposed by the German Wilhelm Wundt (1832–1920), generally credited as the founder of modern psychology. Wundt took an epistemological position, stating that the role of the senses was the primary way that the outside world becomes internalized. The internal world of thought was then formed primarily through interpretation of the sensory data. For Wundt, this allowed psychology to interact freely with anthropological research, in determining the various ways that different societies had constructed their epistemological categories. It also removed any need for discussion of a "soul" or even a "mind" for that matter. For Wundt, mythology was a way that shaped the perception of the world. While Wundt talked in terms of historical and mythic "stages," these were not as strict as many of those posited by the social evolutionists, and he firmly believed that all people had equivalent mental capabilities, simply shaped differently due to their different cultural settings.

While Wundt is more known as the father of experimental psychology, his interest in combining psychology, linguistics, mythology, and anthropology led to the approaches of cultural psychology, psychological anthropology, and various other pursuits. For Wundt, language, myth, and tradition could be viewed through three main psychological processes: thinking, feeling, and motivation. Wundt's efforts were to be carried forth by many students and scholars influenced by his work, including Boas, Durkheim, Malinowski, as well as the pioneering anthropological linguists Edward Sapir (1884–1939) and Benjamin Lee Whorf (1897–1941), who together would produce the important theory of linguistic relativity (otherwise commonly known as the Sapir-Whorf Hypothesis, which holds that the language one uses influences the way one thinks).

Myth as Personhood: The Psychoanalytic School (Freud)

Another scholar profoundly influenced by Wundt's work, who would go on to become much more famous, was the father of psychoanalysis, Sigmund Freud (1856–1939). It is difficult to do justice to the wide range of impacts that Freud had in the scholarly and public imagination, but chief among them were his establishment of psychological principles such as the unconscious, and the role of social repression of individual desires. Although the individual might have impulses of aggression and sexuality, societies sought to harness that, encouraging individuals to repress their emotional states. In turn, societies relied on that repressed energy for building the elements of civilization ("sublimation"). The dance between individual and society, for Freud, was always a difficult one. Most of the cultural influence, Freud believed, was learned during the important and formative years of early childhood. For example, Freud believed that the Abrahamic "God the Father" figure was a reflection of the infant's need for a powerful, protective father figure.

Freud also hypothesized, as did many earlier writers, as to the development of human societies. For Freud, the psychological mechanism of repression and sublimation provided the "origin story" for human culture. The "primal horde," according to Freud, had no laws or rules. The first step toward civilization began with the establishment of the complementary factors of the incest taboo, and the establishment of the institution of marriage. The "Oedipal complex" was held to be the way in which gendered sexuality was established for boys, vis-à-vis the prohibition against incest. For girls, Freud proposed the "Electra complex." Both involved the repudiation of incestuous desires, and the acceptance of a non-incestuous substitute for the original object of sexual desire.

What is striking in Freud's formulation is the way that the conflicts between the person and the society are brought to the fore in terms of understanding not only human pre-history, but also contemporary psychological states. Francisco Vaz da Silva has also pointed out (2007) the various ways in which Freud's version of the human condition relies on myth: from the very naming of the many processes from Classical myths (Psyche, Narcissus, etc.), to the "origin story" he proposed (which tells a story of a mythic struggle against a son-murdering, incestuous ancestral ogre, overthrown at a mythic moment to create modern customs, laws, societies, and individuals). Life lived by rule supersedes life lived by instinct. Even the "Oedipal myth," as it has become known, is a case in point: the story is not really a myth in any sense; it fits more our definition of a tale. But in Freud's hands it has *become* a myth—a central formative story of how we came to be. If the early romantic nationalists were busily creating myths of the nation, then Freud's impactful scheme can be seen as helping create a mythic narrative of the origin of the psychically mature individual.

Extensions of Freudian Thought (Malinowski, Rank, Becker, Róheim)

As in all mythic accounts, however, there can be a problem in cross-cultural applications. Did Freud's schemes accurately reflect all of humankind, or were they more a reflection of the European society with which Freud himself was most familiar? Malinowski challenged the universality of the Oedipus complex, by noting that this was ill-suited to matrilineal societies. In matrilineal societies, it was not the father who was the most important adult man for young boys to consider, but rather the mother's brother, who would be of the same lineage as his sister's son. Still, Freud did base many of his cultural ideas on two important (and rare) examples of universal attributes of all human societies: the incest taboo and marriage. Further, his basic ideas of psychological processes such as the unconscious, repression, and sublimation continue to be useful for many researchers today.

Otto Rank (1884–1939) was one of Freud's closest and most prolific protégés, and his early work on mythology, as in his work *The Myth of the Birth of the Hero*, follows Freudian ideas fairly closely in examining the role of mythology in terms of the world of the young child. For Rank, the myths become not just projections, but also templates of how to move through life: a formulation that had profound impacts on many later writers of myth, such as Joseph Campbell. Yet after breaking with Freud (largely over the role of emotions), Rank went on to focus on other aspects of the human psyche, including the role of fear of death. For Rank, the fear of death was what gave rise to beliefs in an afterlife, and, via those, mythology. This formulation was echoed in later works such as anthropologist Ernest Becker's 1973 *The Denial of Death* and his 1975 *Escape from Evil*.

Another Freudian student deeply involved with myth was the Hungarian Géza Róheim (1891–1953). Róheim began as a dedicated solar mythologist, yet later began to work with Freud and became a dedicated Freudian. Trained as a folklorist, Róheim traveled to Australia to try to test Freud's theories with the Aboriginal peoples there. His fieldwork strengthened Róheim's conviction of the importance of the role of the long period of infant dependency in *Homo sapiens* as helping shape the foundations of human culture. Róheim also believed that important parts of cultural development were introduced through magical, symbolic thinking, stressing a utility for the "primitive mentality" of mythic thought. Róheim introduced the role of "magical thinking" or wish fulfillment, as a primary motivator for both individual psychology and the creation of mythology.

Do Myths Reflect, or Distort, Society? (Boas, Benedict)

Various strands of Freudian theory, especially the themes of the unconscious and repression, contributed to an explosion of interest by anthropological and folkloristic mythologists of the mid-twentieth century regarding the question of whether, or in what ways, myths "reflect" vs. "distort" the sociocultural realities of the societies that tell them. The stage was set for this debate by the massive work *Tsimshian Mythology* (1916) by Franz Boas, based on texts recorded by Henry W. Tate in the Pacific Northwest. In this work Boas attempts to demonstrate the usefulness of myth texts as documentary evidence for ethnographic writing; he does so by first presenting a large collection of Tsimshian myth texts, and then presenting an ethnographic account of Tsimshian based on these texts. Boas says:

> It is obvious that in the tales of a people those incidents of the everyday life that are of importance to them will appear either incidentally or as the basis of a plot. Most of the references to the mode of life of the people will be an accurate reflection of their habits. The development of the plot of the story, furthermore, will, on the whole, exhibit clearly what is considered right and what wrong. (393)

Boas's demonstration is robust and impressive, though one cannot help but note that in constructing the ethnographic account he silently edits out the more fantastical elements related within the stories.

A productive challenge to the "reflectionist" perspective was offered by Ruth Benedict, one of the first generation of Boas's students, many of whom were more attentive to themes of psychoanalytic theory than was Boas. In the introduction to her two-volume *Zuni Mythology* (1934), Benedict calls attention to themes and events from the stories that defy rather than reflect Zuni conventional lifeways and norms. Benedict suggests that such distortive portrayals might serve a "compensatory" function: instead of reflecting social norms, such stories may thwart norms in order to offer a temporary psychological escape from the demands and drudgeries experienced within society. Mythological reflection vs. distortion quickly became a recurrent quandary in mid twentieth-century myth theorizing, analysts sometimes creating and comparing tallies of traits occurring in a particular society's mythology with those occurring in the same society as described by an ethnographer, in order to judge the type and degree of mythic distortion. Theorists of a functionalist persuasion were quick to see how even distortive portrayals of society found in mythologies might in roundabout ways contribute positively to maintaining those societies—by offering a "safety-valve" for periodic release of social frustrations. It is of course possible that mythologies uphold social structure by reflecting norms even while compensating members by offering compensatory flights of fantasy (see Bascom 1954)—although some have pointed out that this combination is all-too-convenient for functionalist analysis (since distortive portrayals can still be seen as socially functional rather than as dysfunctional).

The basic question of reflection vs. distortion in mythologies remains a challenging topic, to be investigated uniquely in any particular society. As we noted earlier, there are numerous possible motives for such distortion. Myths are full of supernatural beings, who may be envisioned as operating by rules alternative to those seen as applying to humans. Myths sometimes present scenarios leading to lessons on how *not* to behave; and in similar spirit, Lévi-Strauss (e.g., 1971) has argued that mythologies sometimes present contrary-to-fact portrayals of social structure just to demonstrate that these would not work, thus ruling out alternatives and affirming that a society must be the way it is. Humor is also a possible motive for distortion, for breaches or reversals of social norms are often, among other things, funny. Lingering archaisms, exotic borrowings, imaginative playfulness, or inclinations to idealize are among other possibilities to be investigated. But among the many claims put forward regarding mythic "distortion," the most radical remains the one at the base of the psychoanalytic tradition: that we should redirect our search for the power-source of mythology—away from conscious social norms, and toward the unconscious and the repressed.

Structuralism and the Morphology of Myth (Lévi-Strauss, Propp)

A very different, yet extremely influential, view of the role of the mind was espoused by the pioneering works of anthropologist Claude Lévi-Strauss (1908–2009). Myths are returned to a position of foundational importance for Lévi-Strauss, in the way that myths for him set the stage for various created ontological categories, creating the backdrop of much of what we call culture.

Originally trained as a philosopher, Lévi-Strauss was introduced into the world of anthropology by his wife, with whom he undertook his first fieldwork in Brazil. Having to flee France during World War II, he moved to New York City, where he was exposed to the American movements in anthropology, still largely spearheaded by Franz Boas. At one meeting in the faculty club of Columbia University, Boas, at age eighty-four, suffered a stroke, and died in Lévi-Strauss's arms. Lévi-Strauss was also influenced by the work of Russian-American linguist Roman Jakobson (1896–1982), who brought with him the foundations of the semiotics approach stemming from the works of Ferdinand de Saussure (1857–1913), the "father of modern linguistics." Semiotics involved the study of signs and symbols, and moved linguistics into the modern realm by stating that words were arbitrary, socially agreed upon, symbols. Jakobson's work involved the role of binary differentiations—this or that, hot or cold—as elemental building blocks of semantic differences. These two aspects—binary differentiations, and arbitrary, socially agreed upon symbols—later became hallmarks of Lévi-Strauss's approach to mythology.

Lévi-Strauss remains a towering figure in anthropology, and it is beyond the scope of this chapter to investigate all of his contributions. Yet his various works were all linked by his overall concern with determining the structural fit of how mythologies, communities, and mentalities are linked together. Turning away from the functionalist schools that sought how myths operated in society, Lévi-Strauss's vision was more encompassing in trying to grasp how myths, societies, and people are operated together. Lévi-Strauss's **structuralism** is an approach to finding the underlying themes at work in the myth. For him, myths were all about the tension between binary divisions in categorical symbolic expression. Lévi-Strauss's structuralism, then, does not examine the structure of the plot in any significant way, but instead proposes to view myth as a discursive source of categorical, and linguistic, distinctions. His ethnographic work shows, for example, how some binary metaphors become important distinctions, as in his examples from South American societies that he discusses in *The Raw and the Cooked*. This is a binary theme that is explored in myth, but also resplendent throughout the languages and cultures as well: people eat cooked food; animals eat raw food. Children are thus "raw" (like animals) and must be "cooked" (instructed, to become humans). Different binaries become important in different societies, and can change, as the societies engage with various structural concerns.

This follows the philosophical ideas of such thinkers as Hegel, who utilized the triadic relation of thesis, antithesis, and synthesis, in terms of logic. For Lévi-Strauss, synthesis was what the myths appeared to achieve: thus the myths were "logical," or rather, the myths set the conditions for logical truth. Further, myths appeared through narration to achieve synthesis, naturalizing the cultural and arbitrary symbolic classifications of the binary divisions, the this and the that, hot and cold, thesis and antithesis. At times this is accomplished by mediating elements within the mythology and the role of the **liminal.** For example, in his study of Native American **trickster** figures, Lévi-Strauss argued that they mediated between two strongly held binary classifications: prey vs. predator. While much of the world was seen in these terms, the trickster, embodied by Raven or Coyote, escaped this binary. Ravens and coyotes are primarily scavengers, neither prey nor predators, and hence their liminal status gives them their very creative role as tricksters.

Lévi-Strauss's work on mythology is notable for the way it brings in multiple strands of scholarship, from anthropology, philosophy, psychology, semiotics, and linguistics, all in the service of understanding the close relationship between myth, the community, and the individual mind. On the one hand, it is a universalist approach, as it proposes the same role of myth everywhere, resulting from human-wide cognitive thought processes. Yet on the other hand, the form that myths will take, and the cognitive categories they negotiate, will be vastly different for different societies. His complex view of myth accounts for long-standing mythic traditions as well as innovation and change; both for evolutionary approaches, and for diffusion; both for universal mentalities, and cultural variation.

Lévi-Strauss's structuralism refers to the structure of cognitive categories at play within mythology—as such, his approach is at times labeled "paradigmatic structuralism." A very different form of structuralism was pioneered by Vladimir Propp (1895–1970). Propp was interested in the plot structures of stories, the syntax of what happens first, next, and so on. Hence his approach is labeled "syntagmatic structuralism." As contemporaries, Propp and Lévi-Strauss engaged in vigorous debates as to the best way to apply structural approaches to mythic narratives. While both Propp and Lévi-Strauss remain influential, Propp's greatest influence has been in the genre of the tale, which supplied most of his data and examples. Mythologies, by contrast, have proven harder to corral into discrete plot structures.

Once More for the Monomyth: Archetypes, and the Collective Unconscious (Lévi-Strauss, Campbell, Eliade)

Other scholars have tended to appeal more broadly to universalisms, without Lévi-Strauss's attention to cultural variation. For the more contemporary universalists, their understanding of myth is often lodged in an appeal to mysticism, religious experiences, and/or transcendental truth. Perhaps for this reason, such approaches have come in for a fair amount of scholarly criticism. Yet at the same time, and perhaps for the very same reason, some of these approaches have proved enormously popular, to the point where there arose in the twentieth century a gulf between the works of the scholarly community, and the public perception of the study of mythology. The idea of the "monomyth," or the idea that all myths are really the same, can be seen as a rejection of scholarly attention to cultural details and variations, as well as a rejection of the rational, empirical basis for scholarship generally. To some degree, universalist approaches are reminiscent of the Church's view in the medieval period: that there is only one sacred story, and any deviations from this are falsehoods. Yet, to another degree, many of the scholars in the universalist schools often take pains instead to paint all mythologies as merely variations of one underlying myth—a tactic reminiscent perhaps of the allegorical school of early Greece, which framed myths as "allegorical" agreements with the world of science. Unsurprisingly, most of the "one true myth" espoused by the universalists seems most closely aligned with the Abrahamic and specifically Christian thought, giving, in a **microcosm**, a reflection of the impact of colonialism generally.

The first, and perhaps most influential, figure to articulate the modern universalist doctrine was Carl Jung (1875–1961), originally Sigmund Freud's prized protégé until his embrace of mysticism and rejection of core concepts of Freudian psychology compelled a decisive parting of the ways. In terms of explaining both myth and man, Jung imagined an unconscious reservoir beyond the individual unconscious: the idea of the "**collective unconscious**" was, for Jung, one of the primary factors that created an individual's psyche. The "collective unconscious" is problematic in that it, like most of Jung's work, is wholly dependent on a mystical, transcendent belief system, rather than empirically based research. While Freud pinned his unconscious on the biological drives of the human animal as repressed by human society, Jung's collective unconscious lies somewhere beyond the individual, and beyond the biological. For Jung, the collective unconscious could be detected in mythology, which he saw as comprised of "**archetypes**"—universal themes that were common to all mythologies and all religious systems. This is also a decided break from the ideas of universal elements of human cognition as proposed by the structuralists (such as Lévi-Strauss), since Jung was not talking so much about human cognition, as about a transcendent phenomenon, interpreted by human cognition. Much of Jung's work dealt explicitly with mystic revelations, and acceptance of his work requires an acceptance of his subjective experiences, rather than a study of objective phenomena. His proposal that "archetypes" unified all mythic action in a transcendent truth has also not been validated by objective research, but instead relies on a singular interpretation of a vastly wide range of mythological figures. Jung remained highly interested in mystic experiences, the occult, and a few divergent religious views—most strongly Christianity, but also Eastern religions such as Hinduism, Buddhism, and Taoism. For Jung, the role of religion was to allow the individual to experience archetypal visions, and to become one with the divine: in Jung's phraseology, this was "individuation."

Jung's views were popularized by Joseph Campbell (1904–1987), who relied heavily on Jung's initial formulation of "archetypes" and the "collective unconscious" for his own bestselling popular works on mythology. It was Campbell who popularized the term "**monomyth**" (derived from James Joyce): the term was, for him, the indication that all mythology is, actually, just one mythology. This is once again the "allegorical" turn, yet with a sweeping dismissal of cultural variation. Campbell's best-known work is *The Hero with a Thousand Faces*, which charts the "archetypal" journey of the hero. His thoughts on the role of mythology as a charter for moving through life are a repetition of those proposed by Otto Rank (uncited), yet most of his "hero's journey" is a distorted recitation of the work of Lord Raglan's *The Hero* (1936) (also uncited) (Segal 1984; see also Dundes 2005). Besides liberal examples of such borrowing and his reliance on the subjective, mystic categories of Jung, Campbell's work is also problematic in that many of his examples for establishing the "monomyth" have very little to do with myth, instead drawing liberally from fairy tales, legends, and popular fiction. His few specific claims of universal motifs have been decisively disproven (Segal 1984, Dundes 2005). Many mythologists, therefore, are skeptical of the scholarly utility of Campbell's work, yet its immense popularity has scarcely been dented.

The popular appeal of Jung and Campbell's universalist and transcendental view of myth can be seen in the wider light of the growth of the celebration of the individual, and a rejection of empirically based rationalism, as well as the ongoing colonialist tendencies to subsume other people's mythic views to that of the dominating society. This problematically allows for a cavalier attitude toward cultural variation and an erasure of important differences between cultures, thus minimizing the understanding of the explanatory powers of mythology.

Jung and Campbell are often liberally utilized by those who approach the study of mythology as a way to reach transcendent truths and religious experiences. Another figure who has similarly contributed the broadened appeal of mythology study, albeit with a much more scholarly approach, is Mircea Eliade (1907–1986), who sought to connect sacred stories with personal, transcendent experiences. While Eliade collaborated briefly with Jung, his own work and theories took him in a somewhat different direction. Eliade approached mythology as a subset of religious experience, highlighting the personal experiential component of mythology. For Eliade, the individual participates in the divine via the performance of rituals, connecting the mundane world with the sacred, the present time with the primordial time of creation, and securing the individual a meaningful place in the cosmos. This nostalgia to experience the time of creation was, for Eliade, the basis for the creation of myths: humans were inherently motivated by what he called the "eternal return" that rituals sought to provide. The absence of myths in modern society, in this view, was not a step forward, but rather a step backward: since myths allowed for people to place their own lives into a cosmically meaningful framework, the absence of such myths left people spiritually destitute.

Similar to Jung and Campbell, Eliade asserted a universal approach to understanding mythology, and believed that myths could reveal transcendental truths, although he stayed far away from claiming any one particular monomyth or underlying archetypes. Eliade has been widely criticized for his lack of attention to facts and ethnographic details, and his quasi-evolutionary schemas are idiosyncratic, and have found little scholarly support. While not often taken as a good guide to mythology in general, some aspects of Eliade's work have been favorably reviewed in terms of some specific mythological traditions, which at times do seem to emphasize, for example, the temporal connection between the contemporary profane and the primordial sacred via the role of myth-rituals.

As suggested, the impact of the idea of the monomyth can be seen as closely analogous to the assertion during the early Christian era: there is only one true sacred story. Likewise analogous, the popularity of this view may have tended to constrict interest in the broader study of mythology, for if all myths are the same, why study more than one? One could conceivably only study one's own mythology, or even (especially for Campbell) popular literature, movies, or comic books—they are all, for him, telling the same story. The sweeping assumptions of universal truths provide few ways forward for research, beyond noting that any new example is "also" an iteration of the monomyth.

Mothers, Matrilines, and Goddesses: The Divine Feminine in Western Approaches to Myth (Maine, Bachofen, Morgan, Briffault)

Besides the idea of the monomyth, and somewhat in opposition to it, is an interesting storyline of mythic research into matriarchy, matriliny, and goddesses. This avenue of research emerged from the anthropological school's quest for understanding the origins and development of human society. When Darwin published the *Origin of the Species* in 1860, creating a new vocabulary for the origins of humankind, anthropologists were already engaged in the overlapping project of trying to sketch the development of human culture. Wedded together, these are often thought of in terms of "social Darwinism," a theory that claims that the militarily victorious societies are "better" due to the idea of "survival of the fittest" and biological evolution. Even today, one hears the phrase "evolution of human society," although it is now clear that social and cultural processes are not the same as biological ones.

Not all early researches into the development of human societies followed this model. Rather, it should be considered that the two discourses, biological evolution and development of human societies, both emerged more or less at the same time, at times overlapping, and at times less so. The year after *The Origins of the Species* was published saw two classic works published in the anthropological vein: Maine's *Ancient Law*, and Bachofen's *Das Mutterecht*. Both works dealt with Roman legal codes in order to tease out kinship structures, which both authors argued were ultimately the key in understanding how humans came to be civilized. This emphasis on understanding kinship became a hallmark of social anthropology, and researches were carried far and wide throughout the world. Maine and Bachofen agreed on the importance of understanding kinship systems in understanding human societies; however, they had radically different visions of what the past trajectory had been.

Maine argued that the establishment of the patriline provided the backbone for the development of civilized society. Bachofen, meanwhile, held that his researches indicated an earlier stage before the patriarchy, that being a matrilineal, and matriarchal, stage. For both authors, this was reflected in their mythologies. Maine argued for the necessary development of patriarchal deities, while Bachofen was convinced that early Roman and Greek law gave glimpses at an earlier world where a matrilineal society worshipped goddesses, or perhaps a singular Goddess.

This interesting divergence of opinions was given further contours by the work from America by Lewis Henry Morgan, a lawyer who had become familiar with the Iroquois system of matrilineal kinship. Morgan's *Systems of Consanguinity and Affinity of the Human Family* (1871) established some of the details of various kinship systems and reinforced the importance of kinship in understanding societies. Influenced by the growing ideas of unilineal stage development (the idea that all cultures go through the same stages of development), Morgan published his magnum opus *Ancient Society* in 1877, where he utilized his knowledge of kinship systems in putting forth his own theory of unilineal cultural evolution (including his famous stages of "savagery," "barbarism," and "civilization"). For Morgan, matrilineal kinship was a universal substage of human cultural evolution, seemingly vindicating Bachofen's work from afar. But Morgan went further in laying the groundwork for vindicating Maine's androcentric views: for Morgan, patriliny, patriarchies, and patriarchal deities were clearly an improvement.

Yet the scholarly interest in the divine feminine continued, at least somewhat as an oppositional discourse to the androcentric tendencies of Western myth and mythography. An influential, if scholarly problematic, treatise inspired by these writers was Robert Briffault's *The Mothers: The Matriarchal Theory of Social Origins* (1927).

(Re-)Enter the Witches (Murray, Graves, Gimbutas)

Following Briffault, Margaret Murray (1863–1963) was the next to embrace this theme. The respected Egyptologist turned her attention to European witchcraft traditions. Inspired by Frazer's work at reconstructing cult activity, Murray combined data of medieval (and later) witchcraft with ideas of earlier goddess worship, proposing that European witchcraft had roots in ancient goddess worship. More problematically, she also proposed that witchcraft as an institution had survived from these earlier times, and penetrated a great deal of English history. While her 1921 *The Witch-Cult in Western*

Europe was written primarily for scholars, her next book, *The God of the Witches*, was aimed much more at the popular audiences. Most of her claims were discounted by later scholars, as well as by many of her contemporaries. The enthusiastic embrace of her wildest suggestions proved somewhat of an academic embarrassment (she was the president of the Folklore Society from 1953 to 1955). Yet, her assertion of a connection between European witchcraft as a practice and as a (mostly feminine-centered) alternative religion proved infectious, and formed the basis for much of modern Wicca. This influence was most keenly distributed through her student Gerald Gardner (Murray wrote the foreword to Gardner's 1954 book *Witchcraft Today*), who both claimed to belong to such a coven, and who became a major architect of later neo-pagan, and especially Wiccan religious movements.

Less on the ritualistic, and more on the poetic, side of things lay Robert Graves, who combined academic, scholarly pursuits of myth with the artistic interpretation of a poet. Like Murray, Graves was inspired by Frazer's teachings. Yet Graves was also inspired by the Anglo-Irish "Gaelic Revival," which reworked many themes from Celtic mythology into literary adaptations. Graves concurred with his forebears such as Bachofen and Briffault that the original worship of Europeans was one of goddess worship, most presumably reflecting a matriarchal and matrilineal society as well.

> Ancient Europe had no gods. The Great Goddess was regarded as immortal, changeless, and omnipotent; and the concept of fatherhood had not been introduced into religious thought. (1955: 13)

Graves has been critiqued on many points of his scholarship, with his largest impact, like Murray, being outside the realm of scholarship, and with the emerging feminist interest in goddess worship and matriarchies.

Perhaps the best known of all researchers was the archaeologist Marija Gimbutas (1921–1994), a similarly polarizing figure. Gimbutas combined linguistics, archaeology, and artistic interpretations to craft her narrative of an essentially matrilineal and matriarchal society existing prior to, and in opposition to, the Indo-European speakers (whom she dubbed the "Kurgan" people, for the burial use of kurgans). An accomplished field archaeologist, Gimbutas was pivotal for many advances in understanding the early prehistoric civilizations of Europe, much of which can be witnessed in her *Bronze Age Cultures of Central and Eastern Europe* (1965).

Her more interpretive work can be seen in three books detailing her view of Europe's pre-Indo-European culture, *The Goddesses and Gods of Old Europe* (1974), *The Language of the Goddess* (1989), and *The Civilization of the Goddess* (1991). As was the case with fellow archaeologist Margaret Murray, the popular interest in her work changed the nature of her audience, and her later works are progressively aimed at a more popular than scholarly audience. Gimbutas's influence can be seen in polarizing, and popularly influential, works such as *When God Was a Woman*, a 1976 book by art historian Merlin Stone, and Riane Eisler's 1987 *The Chalice and The Blade: Our History, Our Future*.

While many of her scholarly contemporaries felt her generalizations were overly broad for the data at hand, and presented problematically and simplistically for a popular audience, more recent genetic research has lent some support to her central view of the kurgan-affiliated groups (now usually referred to as the Yamnaya people) spreading language, genetics, and a patrilineal culture widely throughout Europe over a relatively short span of time.

Given that the research into the divine feminine was often in opposition to the assumptions of universal androcentrism in much of mythological research, there is an irony that Joseph Campbell proved an ardent fan of Gimbutas's work, even providing the foreword to a new edition of Gimbutas's *The Language of the Goddess* (1989) and remarking on occasion how he wished he had been familiar with her work when writing his work *The Masks of God*.

The thread of interest in goddesses, and the divine feminine, has proved a long-standing counterpoint to the general assumptions (as per Morgan) that androcentric religions, and social structures, were inherently better. The thread also stimulated a great deal of popular interest, and even emerging new mythic and religious traditions, most especially noticeably in modern-day Wicca. The popularization of these views has often been held as a scholarly defect, yet these are two different discourses: there have indeed been scholarly insights as to the role of gender in the realm of the divine (and the mundane), from Europe and beyond, just as there has also been expanding popular interest in exploring possible implications of these concepts, for ongoing religious and social transformations.

The New Millennium: Testing Theories, Deepening Understanding

Besides grand theories, detailed scholarly work on mythology has also continued, resulting in an increasing wealth of data, insights, and analyses. In almost direct opposition to the universalists, the scholarly work in recent years has quietly focused on improving culturally specific, linguistically informed, and ethnographically rich studies. More and more data continues to build from a variety of cultures around the world, moving much of mythological research away from the long-standing focus on European prehistoric mythologies. Many of the recent scholarly studies in mythology have resulted from long-term engagements in the field, utilizing participant observation, language skills, and other hallmarks of the anthropological approach. New material on mythology has come from many minority and indigenous groups around the world: no longer linked to representing earlier, primitive stages of all mankind, the newer views reveal unique aspects of many different mythic traditions. Such linguistically and ethnographically informed work allows us to deepen our understanding of why and how myths continue to be such an important part of cultural worldviews.

In some cases, such work adds new information to the world of myths, or supplies local elements long thought to be absent. For example, Barre Toelken's work on the Diné (Navajo) mythology included an overview of some of their hermeneutic traditions, demonstrating a reflexive awareness of their mythic traditions that many earlier writers would have denied. Henry Glassie's thoughtful consideration of Hindu Bangladesh potters revealed the intense focus on material culture in some mythic traditions. In other cases, the careful ethnographies have been useful in disproving claims of universality, or overly broad terminological usage (such as "The Trickster" or "The Flood Myth").

Language, Speech, and Performance (Basso, Hymes)

In general, these fine-grained mythic studies have revealed several important aspects of mythologizing. One of these is the role of language, and, relatedly, translation. Whereas past scholarly accounts were often marred by incomplete or wildly inaccurate translations, many scholars now spend years in mastering languages before beginning to offer insights on the narrative traditions. Keith Basso's work with the Jicarilla Apache is one such example, but there are many more: it is increasingly thought necessary to master the language of the group under study, as well as being aware of some of the difficulties and pitfalls in the act of translation. Translation Studies has emerged as a discipline with many key points for contemporary mythologists. Similarly, many contemporary ethnographers have paid close attention to the role of performance: narrating traditional material—and especially myths—involves taking a social responsibility for the narration. Dell Hymes (1927–2009) labeled this the "breakthrough into performance," separating performative narration from that of the everyday. "Performance studies" has become such a strong, central concern that it at times approaches being a discipline of its own.

Myth as Ideology (Lincoln, Spivak)

Understanding and removing the logical inconsistencies and inherent prejudices embedded in the long story of Western thought has become an important part of recent scholarship as well. As Bruce Lincoln (born 1948), who studied under Mircea Eliade, wrote: "mythology, then is not just taxonomy, but ideology in narrative form" (1999: 147), and he later added that scholarship was myth as well, but with footnotes (1999: 209). Postcolonial writings that examine the impacts of colonial politics and thought have given way to decolonialism—the various methodologies for removing the vestiges of colonial impact in indigenous lives. Meanwhile, taking many of its cues from non-Western thought, posthumanism has sought to reexamine the category of the "human," long held as an innate fact, in the face of evidence from many different mythic viewpoints that do not hold such a construction.

Others have noted the inherent difficult political positionality of various mythic traditions in an age of globalized colonialism. Gayatri Spivak (born 1942) produced a seminal article "Can the Sub-altern Speak?" which makes this point explicitly. Spivak notes how the discourse surrounding *sati* (ritualistic widow self-immolation in India derived from an incident in mythology) has been used by various authority groups to try to assert political legitimacy. The role of the *archons*, the keepers of the archives and the interpreter of myths, is, for her, like Lincoln, inherently a political issue. The concern with the politics of discourse of indigenous and minority mythologies remains a compelling issue for many scholars. As the world globalizes, will the scholarly discourse globalize as well, away from the "dead white men" coterie of previous generations of scholarship, or will the colonial gaze continue to sweep other mythologies under its own convenient ideology?

Fresh Applications for Classic Theories

At the same time of many of these new and innovative outlooks, many of the theories established early on have continued to prove useful—if often in specific, rather than grand, approaches. Myths are often, though not always, performed in rituals. In some traditions, long-dead heroes can at times become divine. In other traditions, great emphasis is placed on the movements of the sun. In others, a need to join sacred time to profane time is enacted via rituals. Rather than seeing any of these as a totalizing theory, the theories from yesteryear instead become a wide selection of tools in the toolkit for the modern mythological researcher, adapted as necessary to the specific field under focus. Not all fields lend themselves well directly to ethnographic engagement, yet most can continue to benefit from the insights gained: for example, the work in Norse mythology has continued to use many of the philological approaches and methods in improving its data set, yet its results are also increasingly informed by the careful ethnographic accounts of contemporary societies and the newer approaches and theories emanating from the fields of anthropology and folklore.

Newer works have also found fresh applications for mythic study by looking at contemporary uses of myth in everything from advertising to popular science to ecology. Rather than seeing myths as something from the past, the performance-centered approaches have reminded contemporary scholars that myth is continuously being put to use, and continuing to shape people's worldviews and daily lives. Not only old myths are used in this way, or even old myths just coming to Western attention: the student of myth might also notice the various new mythologies that are increasingly a part of our modern world.

This chapter has attempted to give a historical overview of the many ways that the word "myth" has been considered, researched, and utilized in scholarly discourse since the days of the ancient Greeks. It is a testament to its resiliency that the word has continued to be productive for so long. If myth is often held to belong to the past, we may note that it is, indeed, an eternal past, one that is perpetually invoked by cultures and peoples. Myth, rather than belonging in the past, is perhaps better viewed as an inherently contemporary activity that continually considers the ancient past ... and, at times, with much to say about the future as well.

Why Study the History of Myth Theory?

In some respects the intellectual history of mythology (in the sense of the study of mythology) is like the intellectual history of any topic: it has passed through different phases in which the various academic disciplines have converged around overarching concerns of their times. For example, intrigued by growing awareness of the variety of the world's peoples and ways of life, scholars of the eighteenth and nineteenth centuries pursued questions of human cultural origins, distribution, and evolution, in which mythology figured centrally; while twentieth-century scholarship shows a rapidly growing interest in the psychological and sociological functions of various human practices and customs, including myth. Such trends do not belong to mythology alone, but form broader currents of intellectual history in which myth scholarship participates.

Mythic narratives and symbols are among the most imaginative and intriguing of human creations, and their origins and meaning are often obscure. This combination of fascination and obscurity, plus a sense that mythologies touch on matters deep and fundamental in the human psyche, have fueled a spirit of extravagance in theoretical speculations about myth that is matched by few other areas of intellectual inquiry—to the extent that the study of mythology at points seems like a new kind of mythology, that is, a parade of imaginative visions into which fervent thinkers pour their values, passions, cosmic yearnings, and ideas about what humanity is, where we came from, and where we are going.

One Theory to Explain Everything?

One manifestation of extravagance in myth theory is a tendency toward monolithism, that is, a hope to find a universal key that unlocks all doors. Especially when the meaning is obscure—no one knowing quite what to make of this story or that image—the situation is ripe for theories that promise to swiftly all end our bewilderment. This is the context in which Friedrich Max Müller's "solar mythology," an epitomizing example of a monolithic approach, arose to prominence in the second half of the nineteenth century. Müller and his followers had incomplete linguistic knowledge and often little or no knowledge about sociocultural contexts of the narratives that confronted them. The recurrence in these sources of themes such as light and darkness was enough to inspire the idea that mythologies must have arisen as archaic poetic responses to the sun, moon, and other celestial phenomena; and that when in doubt one can read an obscure story as a metaphor of such phenomena. The snowballing of this new key to the psychic treasures of human history went so far that one folklorist interpreted Little Red Riding Hood traversing the dark woods as a metaphor of a comet passing through the night sky!

Even though now seen as a rather bizarre chapter in myth scholarship, solar mythology need not be entirely written off. Social evolutionism, which viewed myth as primitive error, was the main alternative to solar mythology in the late nineteenth century, and over against the evolutionists solar mythology kept alive the idea of myth as a kind of poetry. Further, myth is full of astonishing metaphors, and the heavens, and more generally nature, are among the phenomena that inspire such metaphors in myth. But the desire for a single key that promised to unlock everything led the solarists to an angle that was far too narrow. In the following century myth scholars, emphasizing the relevance of mythology to the workings of psychology and of society, showed convincingly that myth is not just about nature, and certainly not just the heavens. Myth is about life, and life is not about one thing or reducible to one analytical approach.

Let us briefly reconsider some of the other monolithically inclined schools of theory that are now viewed by many as passé, but from which we feel that all students of mythology can retain at least some valuable and viable elements.

Dissemination and distribution. For many, the study of distribution and dissemination, notably as exemplified in the historic-geographic method, has come to be seen as an old-fashioned topic, one that is less interesting and important than the psychological and sociological significance of myth. In response, we would point out that to explore psychological and sociological significance, we have to first ask why people tell particular myths, and almost always a significant part of the answer is that they heard the myths they tell (or at least parts of them) from someone else.

In our contemporary world, creativity has come to be strongly associated with the individual, an orientation that, whether or not accurate in relation in contemporary artistry, could easily lead in myth-study to underrepresenting the role of larger and longer social traditions. Very few myths are entirely, or even dominantly, novel creations. In many cases enough variants have been collected to allow a mapping of geographical distribution and possible routes of dissemination. At the very least, studies of distribution and dissemination can pose a corrective to views that overstate the uniqueness of particular narrators or of the repertoire of particular social groups or even societies. Moreover, as we emphasize elsewhere, myths are typically tied to habitat and landscape, and the study of distribution can lead to insights about why a particular story is found in some areas and not others, or to the way a story has adapted to different regions. Finally, myths are interconnected with other aspects of culture and society, and various components of culture and society may disseminate together; study of dissemination may well reveal such interlinkages.

Social evolutionism. Social evolutionistic theories, especially those of the eighteenth and nineteenth centuries, were structured as ladders of human progress, usually with Europeans at the highest rungs and tribal societies at the lowest. Europeans were portrayed as aligned with science, and tribal peoples with myth. Such evolutionistic perspectives are now in strong disfavor, and rightly so, because of their hastiness, the inaccuracies of their "evidence," and their Eurocentric and often racialist bias. But, along with a sense of theoretical inadequacy, declining social evolutionism did leave in its wake an awareness of the importance of various kinds of profound social transformation that have occurred in world history, which still occupy the efforts of many scholars.

Some of these transformations continually to be centrally important to the study of mythology. The development of writing as an alternative to oral communication is one such concern. Increased urbanization that intensified a discrepancy between worldviews and ways of life, contributing to the rise of the idea of "folklore," is another. Besides contributing to the patriarchy/matriarchy debates, Henry Maine, in *Ancient Law,* called attention to a transformation between social orders founded mainly on kinship-relations, on one hand, and, on the other, on individually negotiated contracts (in which kinship, newly restricted to the domestic sphere, no longer provides the skeleton for society as a whole). Nowadays, many people, when they hear "mythology," conjure up that earlier world—a world organized by royal genealogies and families and similarly organized pantheons, such as that of Zeus and his family. The question that Maine's perspective implicitly raises is whether mythology belongs solely to that archaic world. Elsewhere in this book we discuss some of the scholars and perspectives that reject this restriction.

Myth-ritualism. The myth-ritual school, flourishing in the first half of the twentieth century, tended toward the view that all mythology—if not all art and culture—originated in ritual. As with solar mythology, the basic impetus was not entirely wrong: myths are often rooted in rituals, or at least connected to them, and myth-ritualism did a service in calling attention to the connection. Moreover, ritual clearly is a powerful, generative force in religion and society more generally. In an intriguing 1955 article, "The Ritual View of Myth and the Mythic" (in ed. Sebeok), Stanley Edgar Hyman maps out the realms of scholarship to which ritualist perspectives had been or might yet be applied, including various ancient religions, philosophies, and art forms, folk genres, children's games, Shakespeare and other realms of literature, and forms of social organization. Hyman's enthusiastic article was written just as myth-ritualism was at the top of its arc, promising to illuminate everything—which, for most monolithic theories, is also the point at which interest begins to wane, often quite quickly. Some theories of myth die from being shown to be wrong; others bring about their own demise by following in the footsteps (or should we say the flight-path?) of Daedalus and overreaching.

Psychoanalytic theory. When reading Hesiod's *Theogony*, one can contemplate the unfolding of a magnificent cosmic genealogy, full of color, variety, and majesty. Or one can contemplate, instead, the fact that a primordial act that figures pivotally in this unfolding is the Titan Cronus castrating his father Ouranos. The obsessive search for the "repressed" and for sexual symbols in mythologies has sometimes created a weariness with the psychoanalytic perspective, but the fact is that mythologies from many parts of the world contain central episodes of unspeakable violence, horror, humanly dysfunctional relationships, and other unsavory behavior—a fact that is sometimes conveniently overlooked in celebrating the beauty and power of myth. A smattering of more recent analyses, though not necessarily tied closely to the psychoanalytic tradition, have taken up violent themes in myth and ritual; particularly influential are

Walter Burkert's *Homo Necans: The Anthropology of Ancient Greek Sacrificial Ritual and Myth* (1983)—*homo necans* means "man the killer"—and René Girard's *The Scapegoat* (1989; see also 1987). Whatever its weaknesses, the psychoanalytic perspective powerfully called to attention issues that ultimately cannot be ignored in the study of mythology.

So, why study the history of myth-theory? The pat answer to the question *why study history?* is so that we do not repeat its errors. This is important in the case of the history of myth study, for the errors are many, but our answer need not be entirely negative in tone. As suggested in the foregoing, even the myth theories that are wrong are often partly right; moreover, they often involve sophisticated, if too narrow, probings that brings out aspects of mythology we may not have thought of or that suggest better paths for the future. Even the monolithic impulse can have long-term benefits; for in pushing their premises to extremes, theories often reveal their limits, though perhaps more clearly to future generations than to their original proponents. Theories of myth pose provocative questions about origins, human nature, and the human condition, and it is probably fair to say that the intellectual and aesthetic sensibilities that give us mythology are also mixed in with the sensibilities that give us scholarly theories about mythology. An interest in both can easily go hand-in-hand and even add synergy to our study, as though the ambiguous quality of the term "mythology"—that it means both mythic narratives, and the scholarly study of such narratives—is, after all, meant to be.

Chapter 3

Studying Mythology Comparatively

Cross-cultural comparison has long been an important part of the scholarly study of mythology. Why engage in comparison? The fundamental rationale and benefit of cross-cultural comparison is that it allows us to learn more about the nature of mythology and increase our appreciation of it. This occurs in at least four main ways.

The *first* and most obvious benefit of comparison is that bringing different world mythologies into our purview reveals something about the multiple ways in which different humans and human groups have experienced the world, its problems, and its mysteries. Across cultures we encounter a dazzling array of mythological ideas and images portraying how we came to be, how we should live, and what our existence means. By opening ourselves to the array, we develop a feel for the variability, plasticity, and creativity of human psychology and culture. A comparative mythologist's experience can be like that of the biologist entranced at the extravagant variety of life forms in the natural world.

A *second* benefit of cross-cultural comparison, complementary to the first, is that it allows us to explore the possibility of human universals; for while one encounters great divergence in world mythology, one also encounters what seem to be recurrent plots, themes, and images. What to make of and how to account for such recurrent elements, especially when they occur in widely separated parts of the world, is one of the perennial and often contentious questions motivating the comparative study of mythology. A vexing problem in the search for universals is the question of whether recurring images or motifs have the same meaning in different societies; for example, snakes figure in many mythologies, but should we assume in advance their significance remains constant? The safest course is to examine the significance of any element in context—the context provided by both the narrative itself and the society in which it occurs—before leaping to the conclusion that it is "the same" in other societies in which it occurs. A balanced approach, one that is open to both the diversity and unity of world mythology, puts us in position to avoid too-easy pronouncements about "human nature" and to encounter cultural differences in a spirit of tolerance.

A *third* benefit of comparison, one closely connected with the question of recurrences and/or universals, is that it can contribute to our understanding of the historical development and spread of mythologies. One often encounters mythological images, patterns, or motifs that are neither universal nor unique to one society, but are instead spread over a definable geographical region (for example, the North American Southwest, Eastern Polynesia, or the circumpolar north). When joined with other forms of evidence (e.g., linguistic, archaeological, historical, or, more recently, DNA evidence about human settlements and migrations), comparison can contribute to plausible reconstructions of the growth and dissemination of mythologies (and possibly also languages and culture) and/or of the interactions and influence on one another of neighboring societies. It must be quickly added, however, that such reconstructions are susceptible to moral and political pitfalls. Conclusions have often been promulgated prematurely and biased by political agendas, such as twentieth-century attempts, based partly on attempts to reconstruct ancient mythologies, to promulgate the idea of a superior Aryan race.

A *fourth* benefit of approaching mythology comparatively is that comparison can sharpen our experience of any one mythology. Even if a student is particularly fascinated by and devoted to one mythology (Norse, for example), nothing contributes to the appreciation of that mythology's distinctive characteristics so much as comparing it with others. A student can become so immersed in one mythology that he or she starts to imagine that the world could hardly be portrayed in any other way. Comparison reminds that student that things indeed can be otherwise, and at the same time puts the student in better position to notice and appreciate what is unique and distinctive—what stands out—in the particular mythology to which he or she is devoted. Comparison leads one to notice things one may not otherwise have noticed. Even when we are attempting to grasp the character of one particular thing, we generally do so by making tacit or subconscious comparisons with other related things.

An important corollary of this is that comparative mythology allows one to become more aware of the influence of the mythology of one's own upbringing, particularly. When immersed in a mythic tradition, it may at times feel as though one's own mythology is somehow categorically separated from the various other myths the student might encounter during the course of comparative research. Realizing the panoply of myths, and their effects, can help increase awareness of the way in which one's culture, and even psychology, has been shaped by one's own mythic traditions. This is perhaps particularly true of widespread, dominant mythic traditions, such as the Abrahamic. It is easy to fail to assess these in a comparative manner if one has never approached the stories in a comparative framework. Comparative mythology, therefore, holds the promise of not only enriching our understanding or other cultures and peoples, but also of our own, and ourselves, as well.

Comparative Mythology

In the Narrow Sense: The Family Tree

The term "comparative mythology" occurs frequently in scholarly literature, but it is important to be aware of a narrower and a broader usage of the term. In the narrower usage, "comparative mythology" carries the assumption that the mythologies being compared are historically and culturally interrelated as a result of having developed within one language family. A particularly familiar example, one that has produced a large and elaborate scholarly literature, concerns the mythologies that occur within the Indo-European language family. The Indo-European language family is a group of languages (including the Germanic and Romance languages, among others) that, as attested by similar lexicons and grammatical structures, are thought to be historically related to one another, possibly all deriving from a single ancestral language. For some mythologists, the default meaning of "comparative mythology" is this tradition of scholarship on Indo-European mythologies. There are, however, other parallel traditions of mythological scholarship within non-Indo-European language families, such as the Malayo-Polynesian language family of Southeast Asia and the Island Pacific, or among any of the several Native American language families.

Comparative study of mythologies within a particular language family, whether Indo-European or any other, imparts a certain character to the study. In such cases there tends to be a concern with cognate terms and proper names. For example, within the Malayo-Polynesian language family, the central Maori gods of Tū, Tāne, Rongo, and Tangaroa are cognate with the Hawaiian gods Kū, Kāne, Lono, and Kanaloa. When such cognates are noticed, the similarity is assumed to be a result of the historical relation of the languages and their cultures. Comparative studies within particular linguistic families often delve beyond language to encompass a broader concern with the nature and structure of society more generally. Influential twentieth-century Indo-European comparativist Georges Dumézil, for example, argued that the languages and mythologies of Indo-European societies point to a general Indo-European model of society as based on three components or functions (sovereign, warrior, agriculturalist), which are reflected in linguistic terms, mythological pantheons, and aspects of social structure (e.g., the Indian caste system). The same is true in research in other language families; for example, Polynesianists have an interest in indigenous accounts of the original settlement of the islands, aspects of social stratification, chieftainship, oratory, and social customs that are shared with variations through Polynesia.

In the Broad Sense: The World of Myths

By contrast to comparative studies within particular language families, "comparative mythology" when used in the broad sense denotes an approach that admits any and all mythologies to comparative analysis; unlike the narrower usage, comparison is not restricted to mythologies belonging to the same language family. When similarities between mythologies *not* necessarily rooted in the same language family are encountered, different explanations are possible. Historical contact between different cultures and mythologies remains a possible reason for the similarities, for it has been shown repeatedly that stories and other cultural elements pass easily between societies belonging to different language families.

Such approaches can at times be complex. For example, the western Pueblo Native Americans include several languages and even language families, yet share many of the same myths and traditions, including the Kachina spirits, which are found nowhere else. These Pueblo groups share versions of the Emergence myth, in which people emerge from a series of lower worlds, with many others, including the relatively newly arrived Diné (Navajo). Meanwhile, the eastern Pueblo groups follow a different mythic tradition, with people emerging from the water. Notably, the eastern groups are all of the Tanoan language family. Yet, one of the western Pueblo groups, the Jemez Pueblo, is Tanoan-speaking, while mythically aligned with the other eastern groups. In other words, while common language may promote the passage of mythology from one society to another, lack of common language clearly does not impose an impenetrable barrier.

In contrast to explanation through historical contact, the other main possibility is that similarities between different mythologies may have arisen as a result of unrelated societies independently inventing similar plots or hitting upon similar imagery, in creating their respective mythologies. Theories promoting the idea of independent invention are often accompanied by theories about why different societies would independently converge toward similar plots and symbols.

In attempting to account for why different societies might independently arrive at similar scenarios and/or images, one possibility is simply that all humans share a common world and common physical makeup with shared physical, emotional, and intellectual needs. All people recognize the sun, the moon, the stars, water, plants, death, and other inescapable aspects of existence. This at times may make for remarkable instances of convergence: for example, the planet Venus is a particularly bright celestial body. While "Venus" is the name of the goddess of fertility and reproduction in Roman tradition, the planet was also associated with the fertility goddess Inanna from ancient Sumer, and likewise in many traditions in various places around the world. Rather than assume a historical connection between all the stories, it may be easier to follow scholars who have pointed out that the planet Venus is visible (first as a "morning star," and then as an "evening star") for periods of roughly nine months, corresponding very closely to human gestation. Throughout the world, people were likely to have noticed that the planet Venus was visible for the same amount of time as women were likely to be pregnant.

Another example might be the "flood myths" that occur in many societies: an incautious approach might assume this to be derived from a shared historical connection (as the use of the singular term "the flood myth" implies), yet on deeper analysis, the myths are widely varied, and often refer to local landscapes and cultural constructions. Floods can be epochal events for a culture, and have been mythologized by several different groups. The main aspect joining these groups that have flood myths together may be that they are, historically, in areas prone to flooding.

What might look on the surface to be a sure sign of historical connection may, on further investigation, seem to indicate common responses to shared conditions, instead.

These two big possibilities—*dissemination* (whether within or between different languages) through historical contact, on one hand, vs. *independent invention*, on the other—define an ongoing polarity in scholars' attempts to explain the occurrence of cross-culturally similar elements in the world's mythologies. Borrowing terms from biology, the polarity is sometimes expressed through the concepts of "**monogenesis,**" or the idea that a given story originated once and then spread through the world, vs. "**polygenesis,**" or the idea that given mythical plots or symbols have arisen independently multiple times in historically unrelated societies. The polarity has framed a good deal of research and impassioned debate; but much of it is highly speculative and at least some of the contentious issues may never be resolved. In many cases, there could easily be a bit of both, further muddying the issue. Any given myth may have multiple antecedents, all with diverse lineages.

Despite the variety of approaches and the ongoing debate, it would seem that all attempts to account for cross-cultural similarities in mythologies in some way come down to recognition of shared qualities in our experience of being human. As noted, the Jungian idea of archetypes is a particularly radical version of our common humanity, seeing mythological similarities as in-built to the very structure of the human psyche.

At the furthest pole from Jung would lie scholars who reject the theory of such in-built archetypes, who minimize the likelihood of different societies independently hitting upon similar plots and symbols, and who insist instead that cross-cultural similarities should be explained through historical contact and dissemination between different societies. But even this approach implicitly recognizes that humans find new and "foreign" stories interesting and engaging enough to remember and pass them on—thus attesting to at least some degree of common experience between teller and hearer.

Axes of Comparison

In his short work "Categories," the Greek philosopher Aristotle set out a list of ten abstract terms that he saw as useful in differentiating the many things that make up the cosmos and in specifying the distinctive characteristics of each. These Aristotelian "categories" have been recycled many times by subsequent thinkers, mostly famously by the eighteenth-century German philosopher Immanuel Kant, who offered his own version of fourteen such categories. In the nineteenth and twentieth centuries the Aristotelian/Kantian categories, especially in the arguments of French thinker Émile Durkheim, were drawn into comparative sociocultural analysis. We will here propose a comparative grid based on just five of the most important ones: time, space, quantity (or number), quality (or kind), and relation (including causal relations). Since our grid derives from a Western intellectual source, one might be tempted to be skeptical of its use in other regions of the world, but these five categories are so general that it is difficult to imagine a society for which they are without relevance. Further, it should be kept in mind that the grid is not an end in itself, but is merely a provisional device for promoting useful description and comparison, in part by suggesting questions that might be asked. Sources for the comparative examples used in this exercise will be provided at the end of the chapter.

Time

The student new to the scholarly literature on myth is not likely to go very long without encountering the distinction between "**linear**" and "**cyclical**" time. These terms point to a polarity in the attitudes that humans can bring to the passage of time. Linear time is time thought of as a series of unique, non-repeating events, proceeding in one direction only, like the proverbial river flowing endlessly to the sea. By contrast, cyclical time is time thought of as periodically returning to the same point and starting over (which, to continue the metaphor, one could imagine as the sea evaporating and being carried back to the source of the river, to once again begin the journey to the sea). Cyclical time goes in two opposite directions, away from the beginning, but also back toward it. Typically, calendars overlay cyclical time onto linear time; they take a one-way flow and organize it into cycles and cycles within cycles (or epicycles), such as days within weeks within years.

It is important to note at the outset that the two attitudes, linear and cyclical, are never entirely free of one another. For example, linear time, although flowing one way, is typically measured in units that are cyclical in at least the minimal sense of marking generic and reusable periods (minutes, days, years); while cycles, even as repetitions, are also distinguished from one another in terms of their linear order: New Year's 2011 carries different memories than New Year's 2017 does. There has rightly been a tendency to think that myth has a special relationship with cyclical time. This is so for several reasons, most importantly because myth is frequently closely intertwined with ritual. Linking an event or deed recounted in myth to a location on a cyclically organized calendar, as rituals typically do, ensures that it will keep on returning, or that we will keep on returning, to ***illo tempore*** (Latin, "*that* time").

Illo tempore, or a specially marked time in the past, is a frequent attribute of mythology, in terms of both its content and its performance. Myths are often held to be properly performed at specific, recurrent times. These may be life-cycle rituals, such as often accompany births, coming-of-age ceremonies, weddings, and funerary rites, and they may also be calendar rituals, connecting our lived experiences with the cycles of the seasons, celestial bodies, or other phenomena (for example, the Northwest Coast groups often ritualized the return of the salmon in various World Renewal festivals).

The temporal relation between myths and the human world can be, at times, complex. For example, the Dreamtime of many Australian groups is held to be of particular temporal importance. Although traditions may detail the beginning of the cosmos, the emphasis for Australian mythology is centered on the shaping of the landscape, held to happen long after the earth itself was created. This shaping creates a special "mythic time" with profound relevance for humans. The Dreamtime is not only what happened long ago, but also held to be continually happening in a parallel time of our own. Moreover, the Dreamtime is held to be more real than our own time now, representing a sense of cosmic certainty. To understand the Dreamtime, then, is of critical importance in knowing the right way to go about one's life.

Even if linear and cyclical time are never entirely free of one another, mythologies differ greatly in the ways that they emphasize, separate, and combine the linear and the cyclical. Myths also vary greatly in the number of cosmic epochs that they posit. How many epochs are there, and how are they defined? Franz Boas argued that some Native American origin myths show little interest in the ultimate origin of the cosmos and emphasize, rather, a single pivotal contrast between one great period in which the cosmos exists but is unfit for human habitation, and another great period in which, remedied by the actions of a **culture hero**, the cosmos is reshaped in a way suitable for human life. Because of the emphasis on the one-time changeover, Boas was led to refer to such myths as "**transformation**" myths and the hero as a "**transformer**" (by contrast with "creation" myths and "creators"). This is not an idea wholly exotic to Western society; the Abrahamic traditions contain several important mythic moments: not only the creation moment found in the book of Genesis, but also the "flood myth" wherein all living things were wiped out by God, save for a selected breeding pair of each species and Noah and his family. Very often the pivotal events that led to new epochs are dramatized in myths. Christianity often celebrates the birth of Christ as a transformative event in the most sacred sense.

In many mythologies, time is divided into multiple epochs, whose interrelationships may exhibit some larger temporal organizational design. For example, the Native American "emergence" myths of the North American Southwest—those of the Hopi and Navajo, for example—portray humans emerging into this world after spending a period of time in each of three previous worlds underlying this one. The epochs defined by the series of four worlds suggest themes that are both cyclical (since each epoch involves both creation and destruction) and also progressive (since each epoch and its world comes a little closer to what humans ultimately need to live successfully).

Among the Arawakan Wakuénai in Venezuela, there are three post-creation epochs that lead up to the world of today: a rather amorphous (and miniature) early world; a second epoch of the life-sized world inhabited by people, plants, and animals; and the third epoch where people gain cultural knowledge, particularly of shamanism. Each of the subsequent epochs shapes the following ones, and all are brought together in important rituals, suggesting that all three epochs continue, in a sense, in today's society.

Some mythologies ascribe a linearly extended, dramatically deep time-depth to the origin of the cosmos. Polynesian mythologies, for example, do so by portraying cosmogenesis through extravagantly long genealogies composed of beings that embody and personify qualities of privation or nothingness, night, dark colors, and the depths of the sea, followed by searching, churning, gestation, growth, and eventually the first glimmerings of light. These genealogies are performed as chants, the rhythmic cadence and the sheer length of performance serving in another way to artistically dramatize the time-depth belonging to the process of cosmic formation. A sacred character is attributed to the earliest moments because of the power and potency embodied in them.

Time is the most mysterious of entities (or should we call it a substance? a form? a relation?). Time, in conjunction with our fifth axis, relation, gives us relations across time, leading into notions of causation. In thinking backward through the regression of causes by which the cosmos came to be, Aristotle concluded that at some point one must encounter a cause that has no cause—an "uncaused cause." "Philosophical" quandaries about time are found as well in mythologies; Maori cosmogonic genealogists must have something like Aristotle's dilemma in mind when they sometimes append the term *matua-te-kore* ("parentless") to the first element in cosmogonic genealogies, thus suggesting a parentless parent.

By popular connotation, the term "mythology" carries our focus more toward the past than toward the future; we think of stories of ancient times, when the cosmos was first being set up. However, even mythical stories set in the past often, and in a variety of ways, may contain ideas about what the future holds. The fullest versions of this concern are portrayals of grand epochs yet to come, such as the apocalyptic epoch of *Ragnarök* from Norse mythology. The technical term for such concerns is **eschatology** (from *eschaton* or *last time*). But even when lacking elaborate eschatologies, mythologies often relate events or tell of characters who impart specific promises or prophecies that carry us into thoughts about the future.

As alluded to above, one can also often detect a more *general trajectory* associated with the passage of time as portrayed in mythologies. These trajectories can be of several types. At one pole of a continuum would be visions of an original paradise or "golden age," from which all of subsequent time marks a decline. At the other pole would be visions of progress or continuous improvement in the human situation. Perhaps most frequent, however, is some sense of progress and degeneration complexly combined—some aspects of the cosmos getting better while others degrade—or growth and decline combined into some sort of alternating, cyclical relation. But while there may be an overall trajectory to the passage of time, there also may be interruptions and irregularities. Different moments, epochs, or stretches of time, such as the moment or epoch in which a central hero is born, may be marked with heightened degrees of sacredness or with other special qualities that demand our "eternal return" to them, often during sacred rituals.

Whatever the time span depicted in a mythology, things will develop and change; and it is a useful exercise to chart the changes that occur through the course of a mythic narrative. Some changes will involve the physical landscape, whether large-scale (such as the first appearance of dry land from the sea) or small-scale (such as the first appearance of a mountain or bend in the river that will become the defining landmark for a certain human clan). Changes will also occur between different categories of living things, including human beings, non-human animals, and supernatural beings. Humans may lose a primordial ability to understand the speech of non-human animals. Gods may hand over the completed cosmos to humans and then relate with humans only more distantly, or humans may succeed in stealing godly powers. Such changes will often have something to do with the creation of hierarchy, which is one of the persistent motivating concerns of mythologies. Mythologists often bemoan the fact that the distinction between the genres of myth and legend are often unclear, but sometimes myths are quite specific in locating moments of transformation in which gods move to the periphery and humans to the center of the stage, marking a distinct shift between primordial cosmic time and human historical time—to which scholars typically apply the terms myth and legend, respectively.

Most students have heard of the story from Greek mythology of the circumstances that led Persephone to spend half her time in this world and half in the underworld, thus initiating the seasons—the periods of growth vs. those of decay. The mythologies that locate this sort of cyclic time in spatial relations, as per an agricultural metaphor, are often referred to as **chthonic** mythologies (deriving from the Greek differentiation between the chthonic deities of the earth and the Olympian deities of the heights).

In a well-known Polynesian story, the sun travels across the sky too quickly for *tapa* (traditional pounded-bark) cloth to dry properly, so the trickster **demigod** Maui snares and pommels the sun so that it now limps along at a speed suitable to human life. The origin and proper adjustment of the rhythms and cycles of nature (day and night, the seasons, ocean tides and winds) form a favorite topic in mythologies, and colorful examples can be found worldwide. But the establishment of cyclical periodicities is not limited to the natural world: we also encounter numerous stories of godly or human feats or events that become ritualized, as well as stories that directly describe how particular rituals, festivities, or other human customs came to exist, often by the superimposing of humanly important events on to the rhythms of nature.

Time: points to keep in mind
- linear vs. cyclic time
- division of time into epochs
- existence, origin, or adjustment of cycles and epicycles, whether of the natural, supernatural, or human social world
- "creation" vs. "transformation"
- the beginning and end of time (including eschatology, promises, prophecy)
- overall temporal trajectories (e.g., "golden age" and decline; progress)
- *changes* in relationships of humans, gods, non-human animals and other cosmic elements through time
- "philosophical" ruminations, quandaries, and or paradoxes about the nature of time
- sacred or qualitatively special valuations of particular moments, epochs, or stretches of time

Space

Mythologies often contain elaborate and colorful scenarios recounting how the physical layout of the world, from large-scale structures and regions of earth, sky, and sea, to idiosyncratic details of local landscapes came to their present form and/or of how humans came to take possession of these. Scenarios vary greatly.

In terms of macro-layout, in the widespread Native American "earth-diver" myth, for example, the earth in its primal condition is covered with water. A raft with four animals floats on the water, and each of the animal "earth-divers" dives down and attempts to bring some earth to the surface. The final earth-diver succeeds in bringing a mere pawful of earth to the surface, whence it spreads out to form the expanse of land on which humans can live. Earth-diver myths tend not to occur in the same geographical areas as the emergence myths mentioned above; in other words, the two kinds of myths occur in complementary geographical distributions. The reason is perhaps that the two scenarios offer alternative—indeed, mirror-image—accounts of how people and landscape came together. In emergence myths, people come up from below to their present land; in the earth-diver myths, the land is brought up to the people (or rather the forebears of people, namely, the earth-diving animals).

In a scenario spread over a large part of the world we encounter another kind of story of a primordial vertical cosmic adjustment. Specifically, through much of the Mediterranean region, Asia, and the Pacific we encounter cosmogonic scenarios that begin with Sky and Earth as primal parents; and a fair number of these stories include the motif of sky and earth being too close to one other, presenting major impediments to human life. For example, humans cannot stand up straight, so must walk bent over. Then, in a cosmos-shaping heroic act, the sky is pushed up far enough that human life can proceed. A very similar story is told among the Dogon of the North African Sahel, where the heroic act is performed by an old woman, irritated that she kept bumping her pestle on the low-hanging sky.

The three examples just mentioned—emergence myths, earth-diver myths, and sky and earth myths—share an abstract commonality, namely, that the first great cosmos-shaping movement takes place on the vertical rather than horizontal axis. It seems that attempts to conceptualize the highest or deepest forms of sacredness are intrinsically drawn toward the vertical axis (just as the phrases "highest forms" and "deepest forms" draw in vertical metaphors). Perhaps the inaccessibility to humans (until recently) of the sky and the underworld contributes to such a psychological predilection. Mythologies often distinguish more and less sacred locations on the horizontal axis as well, but even such horizontally distinguished regions of sacredness sometimes center on vertical markers such as sacred mountains or underground chambers, or more abstractly on an *axis mundi*, or world axis, running both upward and downward from the earth's surface. In a fascinating book about modern Euro-American middle-class culture as mythology, Roland Barthes (1995) notes that *The Blue Guide*, a travel book about Europe, focuses almost entirely on the vertical—such as mountains and buildings—as sites worth visiting. One might add that, for all their beauty, it is probably fair to say that fewer visitors to the United States come to see the plains of Kansas than to see the Grand Canyon. The topic of vertical and the horizontal in mythology raises the question of human universals. We cannot help wondering about such matters, but should be careful to avoid over-hasty generalizations.

Besides scenarios dealing with the large-scale features of land, sea, earth, and sky, and how these came to their present configuration, mythologies often contain additional episodes that depict the origin of smaller-scale features of landscape: mountains, hills, rock formations, waterfalls in rivers, and so on. The origin of landscape features may be connected with the journey of a culture-hero. For example, Raven, a culture-hero trickster of the North American Northwest Coast, flaps his wings as he flies, and the flapping motion creates the ridges of the Cascade Mountain range, while another Native American culture-hero, Coyote, sometimes adjusts the course of rivers in ways that turn out to be beneficial for humans, such as creating pools advantageous for placement of a fish weir. Aletta Biersack (1999) has documented how, for the Paeli people of New Guinea highlands, the Mount Kare Python forms the landscape, as well as human society, the various neighboring tribes, and the whole local topography. Stories of him not only narrate the fundamental concerns of the Paeli people regarding procreation, marriage, and death, but also narrate the social and physical landscape of the area.

At times, a former giant, or titan, is destroyed, and the destruction and chopping up of his body creates the world, such as we find in the Ymir myth of Norse mythology, where Odin, Vili, and Ve create the earth from his flesh, the ocean from his blood, the hills from his bones, trees from his hair, and so on. His skull becomes the heavens, his brains become clouds, his blood becomes the seas, and his flesh becomes the earth. Such accounts create a homologous relationship between the landscape and human body, a relationship often extended into the social world as well, as in the case of the Mount Kare Python in New Guinea, who creates both the physical surroundings and the various tribal groups living in the area.

There is a commonplace in ethnographic writing that human communities generally regard themselves as occupying the spatial center of the cosmos, but careful analysis reveals that this commonplace is often not quite accurate. The idea of a cosmic center does figure importantly in many mythologies, but human groups often portray themselves as displaced from it, either slightly or greatly. The idea of residing "off-center," and the events that led to that state of affairs, seems to be a highly motivating cultural image, one that dramatizes both the ideal of a perfection to strive for, and the reality of imperfection to live with. Such an image lies behind many of the rituals that we call pilgrimages: these are often built around a journey to a center from a displaced position.

Like the division of linear time into cycles, linear space too is often envisioned to embody repeating patterns, especially in the form of microcosm/macrocosm relationships—or, in other words, patterns that repeat at different scales, from chamber or house to the design of the universe. The most obvious examples are patterns organized concentrically around a given focal point. In his classic work *The Ancient City*, Fustel de Coulanges argued that the Classical Roman idea of a city originated in the organization of an individual household, its hearth, and the family gods of the hearth. The image of the hearth was projected outward from the hearth to the city and indeed the cosmos. Robert Levy (1991) argues that cities are sometimes imagined a *mesocosm* between the cosmos (the macrocosm) and the lives of individuals (the microcosm). Linear and cyclical concepts of space are often complexly intertwined, as when a migrating hero makes a series of stops, and then each stop turns into a radiating center for the teachings or other gifts brought by the hero. Cosmic tiers in the form of upper-worlds, underworlds, or combinations of these may also reveal fully or partially overlapping layouts as well as interesting divergences as one moves upward or downward from one level to the next. The fascination of Dante's *Divine Comedy* flows in part from the poet's deft use of concentric and tiered arrangements to frame the movement of his narrative.

An intriguing image of spatial center and periphery, as well as the relation between ancient and recent time, was discovered by Elizabeth Traube (1986) in her research on Timorese mythological traditions; it is an image that suggests how human communities, their social organization, rituals, and stories fit into a larger whole. Traube found that the Timorese she talked to shared an image of their traditions as making up a tree, with recent local stories as a "tip" of the tree, with the various tips converging into a trunk. Traube's study does not resolve the question of the extent to which a unified version really can be located, but leaves no doubt about the immense power of the image of tip and trunk as an ideal vision that influences social process, ritual, and narrative knowledge and performance in this society.

One of the easiest mistakes for a student of mythology to make is to gloss over the spatial dimensions, directions, paths, locations, and place-names identified or alluded to in mythical stories. Especially when we are reading stories set in places that are unfamiliar to us, it is easy to focus on *what* happens—after all, isn't it the *what* that is important?—and to gloss over the *where*. We should keep in mind, however, that for the creators of mythologies, the *places* described are familiar and themselves carry meaning, often in multiple levels. The landmarks mentioned in mythic stories, even those set in the deep past, may be places that the story-creators see every day in the distance, or return to every year in a pilgrimage, or even pass by every day in their normal routines. Anthropologist Keith Basso (1989) famously described one of his initial encounters with the Western Apache; his collaborator insisted that Basso begin by learning the place-names of the Apache landscape. Basso came to realize that particular stories were so closely attached to particular places, that a mere mention of the place could have an effect as powerful as telling the story. The student interested in understanding a mythic story as fully as possible should consider making a map of the story's setting and research the significance of the places mentioned in the narration.

The stories that make up a mythology can be organized, interrelated, and held together in many different ways: through the logical relationship of the events (e.g., the world must first come to be, before actors can traverse it), through genealogies that show the sequential relationship of characters, through organic metaphors (such as the tip and trunk image mentioned above), or through a hero's life-cycle (e.g., certain events occur in the hero's early life, others in mid or late life); these modes of holding together diverse stories involve temporality. But additionally, stories can also be organized, remembered, and held together by space (A happened here, while B happened here), or by a combination of time and place (sometimes quite systematically, as in a story of a migration with memorable events occurring and various points along the way).

The influential scholar Mikhail Bakhtin (1982) introduced the term *chronotope* (from Greek time, *chronos*, and space, *topos*) to call attention to the importance of time-space conjunctures that distinguish particular narrative genres; by extension, the term might designate particular time-space conjunctures that are created within specific narratives. "Chronotope" was suggested by and loosely recalls the modern astrophysical notion of the entwinement of space and time as "space-time."

Description of places in mythologies can focus on details that are small, irregular, and idiosyncratic; but such details can also coexist with, or fit into, more abstract, geometric notions about the nature and shape of space. Some admittedly speculative examples follow.

Maori accounts of how the landscape acquired its idiosyncratic features are several, and they tend to portray the formation of idiosyncratic landscape features as a de-formation of a more abstract geometric regularity. For example, one account of the origin of mountains and other irregular landscape features attributes these to the pounding from below of the earthquake god, Whakarū-au-Moko. This same god is also god of the tattoo (the god's elongated name is, literally, "Shake-with-Tattoo"), an important cultural practice for traditional Maori and one that introduces a transformation parallel to that worked on the landscape. Specifically, the Maori traditionally used a chisel method of tattooing that created ridges and valleys on the skin, just as earthquakes reshape the "face" of the land, turning a two dimensional surface into a three-dimensional one. On both levels, the landscape and the human physiognomy, a prior plainness and regularity is *re-formed* in order to create important markers of tribal and/or individual identity. Note that these two concerns of the god Whakarū together suggest a different version of the landscape/human-body micro-macrocosmic relation mentioned above in the somewhat different scenario of the carving up of a body to create the world's landscape features.

Various kinds of athletic contests figure importantly in many Native American rituals and myths, where they are often also connected to the origin of the landscape. In Hopi mythology, following the emergence into the fourth world, a pair of youthful culture-hero twins play a traditional ball-and-stick game on the surface of the fourth world. Their playing of the game firms the earth up and seems to contribute to the ideal of a quadrangular shape to the area of human settlement, with four mountains defining its coordinates. The quadrangular landscape thus also forms a macrocosmic parallel of the ideal of the rectangular village plaza that figures in Pueblo architecture. Importantly, the kiva is a subterranean ritual space in the middle of the plaza. Rituals are performed here, completion followed by a departure upward in accordance with the central emergence myth. Both the quadrangular landscape and the construction of the kiva at the center represent the sacred importance given to the number four in Hopi (and many Native American) societies, which is held to be related to the four cardinal directions, with the sacred number five represented by the center, the vertical axis.

The directional scheme that one encounters in the higher volcanic islands of the Pacific offers an interesting alternative to the quadrangular directional scheme just mentioned. Geologists refer to the form of these islands as inverted "cones," and it would appear that the indigenous peoples had something of the same idea, for direction is conveyed not in terms of a square grid, but by degree of mountainward vs. seaward and by "pie-slice" divisions of the cone defined by valley ridges running seaward from the center. This directional scheme appears in traditional narratives and land divisions as well as ongoing ordinary life.

Time and space are often co-invoked in many mythic traditions. In Ireland, the numerous megalithic mounds are said to be portals into the Otherworld of the dead, where time runs differently than in our own. This is particularly true at seasonal nodes, most notably at Halloween and May Day, when the spirits of the Otherworld can freely mingle with living humans in this world. These sites, then, represent a sort of spatial-temporal node between this world and that of the Otherworld.

More abstractly, philosophers have often commented that, although necessary to distinguish, time and space are somehow intimately related, such that we often talk about one with terms borrowed from the other (e.g., a "length" of time). This situation seems not to be limited to "Western thinking," and holds out a question to ask in assessing any mythology: are there terms or metaphors that unite or cross over and/or connect talk about space and time? Regarding asymmetries between time and space noted by philosophers, the most interesting is that space seems to be crossable bidirectionally more easily than is time; or to put it another way, time seems to be more unidirectional than is space. Although we can "go back in time," we seem not to be able to do so in the same easy, prosaic way that we can spatially travel back and forth between two towns. Instead, to go back in time we have to leap from mundane life to another level of experience—that of memory, myth, or ritual—to make the journey back, and to retain our connection to mythic moments. Whether such a formulation holds up cross-culturally offers an interesting question for the student of mythology to think about.

Space: points to keep in mind
- significance of all spaces and places mentioned in narratives
- association of particular stories with particular place (place as a story-mnemonic)
- origin of spatial layout of cosmos and of particular locales
- origin of spatial distributions of people, non-human animals, and other entities of the cosmos
- centers, off-centers, concentric regions, or other forms of macro-microcosmic relations
- contrasts, connections, or cyclical oscillations between linear and concentric space
- mention of or allusions to geometric forms or regularities, contrasts of geometric and idiosyncratic space

- cosmic levels or tiers (upper-worlds, underworlds, how many, how arranged?)
- chronotopes (or important conjunctions of time and space)
- methods of indicating spatial directions
- values attached to different spaces, places, and directions, including horizontal and vertical axes
- images (e.g., tip and trunk of tree) that characterize space and spatial distributions
- spatial metaphors of time and vice versa

Quantity (Number)

Numbers, as well as other terms or images that indirectly or impressionistically suggest quantity, occur frequently in mythologies, figuring importantly in several different ways.

The first point to be aware of is that various cultures have posited particular numbers as special and/or as sacred. The idea of one-ness is a recurring mythic theme, carrying associations of a time before differentiation and differences. The logical contrast to one-ness is the number two, and many traditions place an emphasis on dualism, such as the Dogon, where everything numinous is represented as having a "twin" or counterpart, and the birth of human twins is highly celebrated as auspicious.

A familiar illustration of one-and-two is a scenario, cross-culturally recurrent though not universal, that tells of sex and sexual desire originating from an entity that is originally androgynous but at some point split in two. One of the best-known examples is the story narrated by Aristophanes in Plato's *Symposium*; in this account, Zeus, fearful of the power of the original round, androgynous, four-handed, four-legged humans, decides to split them in two to weaken them—and since then, each half has yearned to rejoin the other.

Mythological characters may exhibit other characteristics that are dual or multiple—perhaps not surprising for beings believed to oversee or summarize the entire cosmos. Ambiguously quantified entities can express particularly profound dilemmas and motivations. For example, what could be a more appropriate image of the enduring conflict of good and evil, celebration and suffering, in the world than a cosmic being or creator who is one but also two, representing both sides of human experience. Twins are encountered often in mythology, and they often convey duality in the form of asymmetry; of the Hopi twins mentioned above, for example, one is more a shaman and prankster, the other more a warrior.

In the myths and tales of Europe, threes predominate (three siblings, three trials to be overcome on a journey, three types of gods) while in Native American mythologies fours predominate (as well as fives, which are viewed as 4 + 1, very often the four cardinal directions plus the center). In these two cultural areas respectively, different numbers signify completeness. Particularly telling and charming examples are found in tales of European origin that have been collected from Native American storytellers; among other changes, patterns of three have sometimes been modified into patterns of four. Likewise, similarly processes of translating Native American myths into English also translate patterns of four into patterns of three. Although threes and fours offer the most obvious examples, they are far from exhausting the numerological patterns found in these societies and their narratives.

A further consideration is that some mythologies strive to convey a sense of the sheer plenitude of the cosmos, either through ordinal or cardinal numbers, or, less directly by other means, such as litany-like lists. Examples of the later are found in Hesiod's poem *Theogony*, which attempts to show how major and minor gods of the Greeks fit together in an encompassing genealogy. In Book 4, for example, Hesiod offers long lists of gods and other mythological characters associated with the sea, the descendants of Pontus (Sea) and his son Nereus (the "old man of the Sea"). Hesiod's tone, but also the sheer quantity of names, leaves one with a feeling of the immensity and importance of this part of the cosmos, and a (mostly) warm feeling toward it and its denizens. In Hesiod's poem, such displays of plenitude are further intensified by the fact that the beings that make up the living physical world all derive from one original parent (Gaia). The genealogy that begins with Gaia thus expresses simultaneously the plenitude and unity of the physical cosmos.

Indeed, the concern to show the unity amid diversity seems to be a concern of many mythologies, one that manifests itself in ways that may be less obvious than the image of a genealogy. A process of "separation" occurs in some mythologies; the origin of the sexes from an original androgyne, and the dismembering of a body have already been mentioned. But a process of separation may also be suggested more abstractly, as in the biblical Genesis account of the Creator separating light from dark, waters above from waters below (placing a firmament or dome between them), or the waters below being gathered to one place so that dry land can appear (Genesis 1:19). In such cases a sense of unity is imparted through a sense of the interrelated origin of the different parts. Not all creators are portrayed as possessing omniscient knowledge; sometimes creators must try multiple times to successfully produce the entity they have in mind. In such cases the cosmos may amount to a sort of inventor's workshop, strewn with failed attempts to actualize one idea. Such multiple failures may, in a roundabout way, impart a sense of cosmic oneness through the *unitary intention* that has produced them; and, further, the varying degrees of successful realization amounts to a cosmic hierarchy of perfection. Among several groups in the Amazon, species of monkeys were former humans who refused to feed a deity, and in punishment were transformed, with humans being instructed to eat them, instead. These examples, then, and no doubt others, suggest that mythologies can seek to affirm not just the diversity of the cosmos, but simultaneously its unity—the unity of the "one and the many."

A fourth quantitative factor to be considered is whether a mythology displays an overall pattern, or specific moments, of either increase or diminution. Norman O. Brown (1985: 16) describes Hesiod's *Theogony* as exhibiting an "evolutionary proliferation."

In the course of the poem the cosmos goes from a few original entities to a bulging inventory. The overall pattern is one of increase. The anthropologist Claude Lévi-Strauss, however, has discussed some scenarios, drawn from several parts of the world, in which mythologies portray significant depletions in content. One of his examples is a Tikopian myth in which a trickster stealing original foodstuffs for humans loses all but four items. Lévi-Strauss argues that such scenarios, in which an original plenitude is depleted, serve to dramatize the few items that remain, as though allowing them to stand out by creating empty spaces between the remnants. In the Tikopian myths, the four remaining items dramatize the Tikopian social system, which is based on four main clans. One can think of many other instances of depletion recounted in mythologies, including peoples and important sacred objects lost in migrations or by disasters such as deluges. Going back to Brown's "evolutionary proliferation," we can add that some beings produced within this proliferation are at some point, and especially with the defeat of the Titans, forced into the underworld, so that at least one portion of the cosmos—the region in which humans live—takes shape not only through a process of proliferation but also one of depletion.

Narratives telling of the depletion of the visible part of the cosmos through population displacement are not limited to Titans and Olympians, but have arisen in human communities in which Christianity displaced prior religious belief systems. The Yoeme, a Native American community straddling the Mexico-US border, recount that when their ancestors decided to convert to Christianity, those who chose not to go along resettled, or, in some accounts, moved into the sea or underground where they still live. The account is at least loosely reminiscent of some accounts by the Irish of the origin of the Fairy Folk (Irish: *sí*): the most famous story is when St. Patrick was preaching of heaven and hell, the fairies asked what would happen to them at the end of the world. St. Patrick replied that they would go to neither heaven nor hell, but remain in the earth instead. When some Tikopian Pacific Islanders decided to convert to Christianity, the missionaries tacitly agreed that they would not dishonor the previous gods; and a new group of stories arose detailing the consequences wrought by the old gods when they are dishonored, implying that they are still there. In such cases one senses a cosmos that is in some way depleted yet in another way made fuller by a less visible surrounding presence.

The most obvious instances of number in mythology lie in the occurrence of actual ordinal or cardinal numbers; but quantitative concern can also be expressed through more impressionistic quantitative terms such as "tiny," "vast," "innumerable," "in an instant," "endless," and also through intriguing and powerful images. Consider for example, this passage in Hesiod's *Theogony*, which combines time, space, and number (specifically nine, also the number of Muses told of by Hesiod) to describe the depth at which the pit of Tartarus sits in the underworld:

> A bronze anvil falling from the sky would fall nine days and nights, and reach earth on the tenth; a bronze anvil falling from the earth would fall nine days and nights and reach Tartarus on the tenth. (Hesiod 1985, 73)

Even though we may think of counting as a rather prosaic act, important recurrent or perhaps universal psychological proclivities may be approached through it, leading into the next category we will consider, "quality" or "kind." How many basic categories of things does the cosmos contain? Are there specific conditions or situations that lead cultures toward "lumping" (that is toward big, inclusive categories) or, conversely, toward "splitting" (that is, toward finely gradated categories)? Are categorizations built from the top down, the bottom up, or upward and downward from a mid-ground? Cultural anthropologists, linguists, psychologists, and cognitive scientists often broach such questions, and it would seem that mythology offers a prime source of evidence for such interests.

Quantity: points to keep in mind
- narrative occurrence of ordinal and cardinal numbers, and their significance
- lists, terms, or images that convey quantity impressionistically or indirectly
- numbers that are special or sacred to a particular society, explicitly or implicit in patterns of repetition
- deities or other beings that are quantitatively ambiguous, and their significance
- means of conveying plenitude, unity, duality, and their interrelation
- patterns, or focal moments, of increase, depletion, or displacement, how these arise and what they mean

Quality (Kind)

By quality we mean the properties that distinguish any particular identity, those distinctive characteristics that define particular "kinds" of things over against others. Quality figures importantly in mythology, and it is possible to sketch some of the more recurrent ways.

The first and most obvious emphasis on quality consists in juxtapositions of sensory opposites. The biblical Genesis origin scenario provides a ready example, specifically the separation of land and sea and other creations described as involving separation. The anthropologist Claude Lévi-Strauss gave particular emphasis to the way that myths invoke sensorily experienced opposites to convey important messages about the nature of culture and society. Most famously, he argued that widely spread stories of humans acquiring cooking fire portray the origin of society and socialized human behavior through a contrast of cold, raw food vs. warm, cooked food. Coldness correlates with pre-social existence, warmth with social existence. Directional systems of the Native American peoples of the North American Southwest often associate the four directions with contrasting colors. Colors themselves often reflect mythological categories, with various chromatic symbolisms linking myths and various aspects of everyday life (e.g., white as representing purity or goodness).

A second way in which mythologies emphasize qualitative differences is by juxtaposing a general condition of cosmic disorder, sponginess, or blurriness to a cosmic state of order, firmness, or clarity. To invoke the Genesis myth once more, it is not just that light comes to be distinguished from dark and sea from land, but that in a more general way order comes to be distinguished from disorder: the ordered world at the end of the creation story stands in opposition to the opening of the story in which chaotic, formless waters prevail.

One of the most striking scenes in Hesiod's *Theogony* is the battle scene of the Olympians and Titans:

> If Earth were being smashed and if Sky were smashing down upon her, the noise would be as great as the noise that arose when the gods met in battle. The winds added to the confusion, whirling dust around together with great Zeus' volleys of thunder and lightning-bolts, and carrying the battle cries and shouts from one side to the other, so that the uproar was deafening. (Hesiod 1985, 73)

The power of the scene derives not just from the thrilling action, but also from the contrast the chaos of battle offers vis-à-vis the process of Zeus imposing a new order on the cosmos immediately following the triumph of the Olympians; the battle and its aftermath form yet another version of the passage from chaos to order.

A third way in which mythologies emphasize the qualities of the diverse things of the world is by offering colorful and memorable tableau scenes in which the distinctive qualities of different kinds of entities of the world shine forth. The cosmogonic account of the Jicarilla Apache, for example, contains an episode of a primordial race around the entire world in which all living things take part; the account emphasizes the different modes of locomotion—running, flying, crawling—and creates in the hearer's mind a spectacle of the richness of the living word based on modes of mobility—a fitting outlook for a group whose language is particularly rich in a verbal system centered on motion and activity, as opposed to the static sense of noun-centered languages. Human runners each year ritually reproduce the primordial world-around race in microcosm by running a race between the starting and ending points of that first world-defining race. The emergence myths mentioned above sometimes offer an equally powerful spectacle, by suggesting that the living things that will comprise the fourth world emerge on the stalk of a plant, arrayed from the bottom to the top in a sort of vertically oriented parade; the original emergence journey too has a microcosmic counterpart as dancers, in colorful and distinctive costumes, nowadays emerge from underground ritual chambers (kivas) to begin ritual dances.

Qualities of course are defined by contrasts with other qualities; but there is also a sense in which, more abstractly, quality might be set in opposition to quantity—specifically by overriding the latter. For example, in the earth-diver story mentioned above, earth comes into being when one of the diving animals succeeds in diving far enough down to retrieve a pawful of earth from the floor of the ocean. It is notable that such stories often seem not to fret greatly about how a mere pawful of earth can supply the mass of land on which we live. It is as though once we acquire the *quality* or the distinctive essence of something, the quantity necessary for life will take care of itself. In some examples of quality taking narrative precedence over quantity, a principle of contagion may be involved; we know that fire in certain conditions spreads by itself, a tiny spark turning into a conflagration; and, perhaps like airborne illnesses, once Pandora lets the evils of the world out of the jar, evil or mischief is then a possibility everywhere in human life. So perhaps what is involved in the earth-diver myth, and others like it, is a transference of the contagious character that we experience in some substances to other substances that we normally do not think of as being contagious, such as land.

But whatever is behind such scenarios, the overriding of a quantitative by a qualitative focus provides one more way in which the distinctive qualitative characteristics of the many elements that make up the cosmos are dramatized.

The four strategies just considered—certainly others are to be found—are ways in which the qualities of the cosmos are explored and highlighted in mythic narratives. These examples all suggest an impetus toward classifying the cosmos, but sometimes mythologies draw upon even more explicit markers of classification. The importance to many mythologies of genealogy has already been noted, and here it should be emphasized that genealogies are classifications and that classifications are inherently hierarchical, placing some categories as superior to, and encompassing of, others. In Hesiod's genealogy, various of the Titans are associated with different groups of beings, becoming tutelary deities (e.g., Okeanus of water-beings; Hyperion of beings of the sky and horizon). Senior lines of descent give rise to those who want to maintain the established order, while junior lines give rise to the rebels. Parenthetically, in assessing the genealogies that occur in mythologies we should not be locked into concepts from Western biological science, but should attempt to uncover, rather, the principles by which any particular mythological genealogy itself is constructed. For example, some Maori genealogies posit birds as the children of trees and insects as the children of plants, which differs from the Western biological account. The aspect of parentage Maori genealogies emphasize is the offering of protection and a home, an aspect fully consistent with Maori mythology's portrayal of Earth as the parent of human beings. Among many Northwest Coast groups, different clans are associated with different totem animals, all with different mythological roles, implying social relations between the various lineages in accordance with the mythic traditions.

One should also be aware that the things of the cosmos can be subject to multiple classificatory schemes: in some cases, these amount to overlapping taxonomies constructed for different purposes or from different points of view; in other cases they may be hierarchically ordered as multi-tiered taxonomic grids. That is, one may encounter grids that take already-classified entities and arrange these under one or more levels of supervening macro-categories, such as masculine vs. feminine (as some languages do for nouns), or sacred vs. profane. A **"moiety system"** is a form of social organization in which all members of a society belong to one of two halves of their society (and generally are required to take their spouses from the opposite moiety); some anthropologists believe that there is evidence for this form of social organization through much of the world and of human history. What is important here is that some societies based on moieties regard these opposed units as encompassing not only all humans but all entities of the cosmos: whatever its other classifications, everything in the cosmos is also either an "A" or a "B."

Numerous mythological stories are inspired by some sort of classificatory incompatibility or anomaly. We have mentioned the genealogy of physical earthly things that derives from Gaia in Hesiod's genealogy. But Hesiod's poem also contains a second genealogy that derives from Chaos, whose descendants tend to be conditions and/or psychological states rather than physical things; they include Night, Retribution, Famine, Sorrow, and Madness, among others. The descendants of Gaia and Chaos never intermarry, as if to say the cosmos is dualistic, composed of two incompatible macro-categories of entities forever at odds with one another.

In some ways similar, while in other ways opposite to the foregoing, is the view that discrete things contain their opposites. The psychologist Carl Jung (1977) explored this pattern (which he termed *coniunctio oppositorum* or "unity of opposites") in a range of mythologies and especially in medieval alchemy. Gold is gold and lead is lead; one is bright and shiny, the other gray and dull. But, according to Jung, alchemy rested on the belief that each of these discrete elements contained the other, its opposite; and he argued that similar beliefs are found recurrently in world mythology. The caution to be taken here is that the classifications found to inhere in mythologies should not necessarily be taken to imply that entities of different kinds do not interpenetrate or intermix with one another.

Moreover, systems of classification or taxonomies almost always produce anomalies—beings that do not have an easy fit. Apparently because they share characteristics of both land- and sea-dwellers, Maori mythology recounts how a group of beings from the genealogical line of fish, through either confusion or discord, ended up on land: these are the lizards. Mary Douglass (2002) and other anthropologists think that such "interstitial beings," those that somehow fall between categories, are particularly good candidates for possessing a powerful and/or threatening status. This brings us to the idea of the "liminal": the category of places, beings, and times that lie in between the categorical distinctions. The liminal is "where the magic happens," in that it refers to the areas of anomalies, which retain the power for threatening or overturning the usual categorical distinctions. The character of the "trickster" is often derived from its liminal position.

Although differently constructed in different traditions, tricksters are by their very nature subverters of the established order. The characters that mythologists label as tricksters typically combine opposite characteristics: seriousness and buffoonery, naivete and wisdom, age and youth, selfishness and altruism. Such beings may defy classification, yet arguably their creative power also depends on the existence of the classificatory principles they confound.

Quality: points to keep in mind
- juxtapositions of sensory opposites (e.g., hot-cold, light-dark, rotten-fresh, wet-dry)
- juxtaposition of general conditions of disorder and order
- tableau scenes that dramatize distinctive qualities of different entities
- genealogies as classifications; the principles through which genealogies are constructed

- the classifications imposed through any other methods or forms of hierarchy
- classificatory anomalies (i.e., entities that do not fit) and their stories; special powers that might derive from anomalous (interstitial, liminal) positions in classificatory systems
- unities of opposites (i.e., beings that combine opposite qualities) and their stories, including "tricksters"
- multi-tiered classifications (for example, the duality of moiety organization overlying more specific categories)

Relation/Cause

In the broadest sense, "relation" refers to the fact that the different entities that make up the cosmos for the most part do not exist in isolation; rather, they are linked, often in multiple ways that allow them to interact and influence one another. As used here, "cause" is a subset of "relation"; it denotes, more specifically, the power of an entity to exert a shaping or controlling force on another entity or other entities. Perhaps the safest assumption is that the student of mythology should be ready to encounter, in creative and unexpected applications, the full range of forms of connection and entanglement, of attraction and repulsion, and of motive force and resistance to it, he or she sees operating in the ordinary world—and then some. The powers that propel nature, including volcanism, weather, and organic growth, are tapped as motive forces of cosmogenesis, but so are the myriad forms of power and influence that we encounter in everyday human interactions. That is, as noted elsewhere, mythologies often anthropomorphize nature, thus tapping something like human intentionality and willfulness to account not just for human life but also for the origin and workings of nature.

A good starting point is to ask: what kinds of powers are depicted in a given mythology, and how are such powers distributed through the cosmos? In many mythologies, the forces that shape the cosmos involve some sort of power of will. Some creators are omniscient in having both perfect power and perfect knowledge, but perfect knowledge or perfect power are each possible without the other, with interesting results.

Other creators or transformers are neither omnipotent nor omniscient. Creation or transforming of the cosmos in some cases amounts to an experiment or even an accident—a naive, first-time event whose outcome is uncertain. Native American tricksters such as Raven and Coyote often act on innocent, unrestrained impulses with mixed, unanticipated, and/or sometimes humorous cosmos-shaping results. Motives for creation are also many. In mythologies one encounters beneficent motives, but also less beneficent ones. The self-interested acts of creators sometimes have positive consequences for humanity.

Acts of revenge or retribution are common in mythologies; in Hesiod's *Theogony*, for example, they often take on a cyclic, generational character, each act of retaliation inviting another, and each spawning new alliances and/or intermarriages. Yet the pattern of retributions, emanating from the wills of individual protagonists, does not exhaust the motive force of cosmogenesis in the *Theogony*, for at least two other manifestations of motive force can be seen. One of these is procreation, for the *Theogony* is one of many mythologies in which cosmogenesis proceeds through mating and birth. Besides Gaia and Chaos, who give rise to the two genealogies that together make up the cosmos, Hesiod names a third original entity, Eros or desire, which does not beget a genealogy but seems rather to points to one fundamental level of energy that propels cosmogenesis. The sexual-reproductive genesis of the cosmos inherently implicates gender relations, which in the *Theogony*, and indeed in many mythologies, is complex and should be analyzed in detail in considering the cosmic distribution of power. In the *Theogony*, the female protagonists are indeed powerful, although after Gaia (who produces Sky, Mountains, and Sea parthenogenically and "without the passion of love"), their power, as the narrative progresses, is increasingly, though with some exceptions, exercised through background strategizing and contrivance.

Although the image does not figure importantly in Hesiod, it should be recalled from comments above that other mythologies propelled by sexual reproduction, such as some of those found in Polynesia, draw in other images of organic growth, including growing plants and spreading vines or trees. Such images tap a general power of growth comprised in the living world.

In recounting Prometheus' success in tricking Zeus, Hesiod says that Zeus was never really deceived by Prometheus, but rather decided to allow Prometheus to succeed in his machinations. This comment, along with others, suggests that beyond the play of individual wills engaged in strategies of retaliation, beyond the power of procreation, and beyond the power of growth embodied in living things, Hesiod is striving to add yet another motive force of cosmogenesis: that of Zeus as an omniscient deity. Hesiod seems intent to shift the power of the cosmos toward Zeus, and in general it should be recalled that many power shifts take place in mythology, and take many forms, including, among others, conquest, theft, trickery, and sometimes voluntary handoffs of power.

Western students of mythology will usually come to this study already familiar with worldviews that attribute power and will to gods or other supernatural beings and to humans. They may be less prepared for worldviews that attribute human or godlike will and power to non-human animals or to other entities of the natural world, such as trees, plants, and rocks—worldviews in which, in other words, power is more widely distributed through the cosmos; but there are many such instances to be seen. In one version of Maori **cosmogony**, a set of sons born of Sky and Earth are attacked by a god who represents wind and storms. Some of the sons want to remain on the land, but one wants to take his chances in the sea. The land and sea groups part in mutual scorn. The logic of the story seems to be less that one of the sons is Fish and therefore goes to the sea, than that this son decides to live in the sea and therefore becomes

Fish. Species and their characteristics, in other words, arise, in part at least, from the inner willfulness of the different species of the natural world.

A different kind of example is found in Native American mythology, in the frequent occurrence of stories of intermarriage or adoption between humans and members of non-human animal species or other elements of the cosmos such as stars (the widespread "Star-husband" tale, in which two human women decide that they want to marry stars, and do so). Throughout North and South America, one finds such stories of humans intermarrying with or being adopted by other natural species, whether bears, jaguars, or snakes. Given the contemporary interest in sexuality and gender in Western academia, one might be inclined to consider such stories in this light; but the stories themselves seem more concerned to explore and elaborate upon the types of social benefits, responsibilities, and obligations that go with this form of interrelationship. In an important sense, stories of intermarriage are similar to stories of adoptions: both result in children who belong to two different groups, creating a bond between them.

Such stories pose a highly reciprocal relationship between the two different-species spouses, each spouse (and their relatives) having specific things they want to gain, as well as specific things they owe, through the relationship. Such stories often describe humans acquiring valuable qualities and power from the other species. It is interesting to note that the great boon of controlled fire that Hesiod depicts humans as acquiring from the gods is acquired in some Native American accounts via intermarriage or adoption or sometimes by theft, from a non-human animal species who first possesses it. Such stories also portray a cosmos in which value and power are distributed among different species rather than centered in one.

A bit more abstractly and technically, we might say that a recurrent theme in Native American mythology is human relationships to nature sometimes portrayed through affinal rather than consanguineal kinship—affinity being the technical term for relationships through marriage (i.e., in-laws), consanguinity for relationships through descent or "blood." In Hesiod's *Theogony* and numerous other Mediterranean and Asian mythologies, human relationships to other realms of nature tend to be portrayed consanguineally—one line of descent leading to celestial phenomena, another to water creatures, and so on; and long genealogical lines of descent going back to the origin of the cosmos are often adduced by human rulers to legitimize their claims to power. What should we make of the fact that Native American mythologies more fully explore affinal links in portraying the human place in nature? On one hand, consanguineal links might seem to be more inalienable than affinal links, but on the other hand, affinal links, just because more fragile, create an emphasis on mutuality and reciprocity; both sides must contribute if the relationship is to endure. There is much more to explore, but suffice it to say that it is not enough just to say that kinship figures importantly in many traditional mythologies—that much is obvious. Kinship is complex, and we must more deeply look into the *particular kinds of kinship connections* that different mythologies explore, not just for the purpose of creating human social structure, but often also for portraying the human place in the larger world of nature.

Among many West African groups, such as the Fon, there is a combination: the creator deity Mawu traveled together with Aido-Hwedo, the Serpent, to fashion the landscape from the Serpent's actions. Mawu and her consort Lisa form a duality, associated with both the sun and the moon. The offspring are all important, but the most important is Legba, who acts as the messenger of the gods. Linked with the complex panoply of demi-gods and creator divinities are practices of worship often of a divinatory nature. To know the gods is to know the future, in such traditions.

Whatever other forces may be present, humans will want to be apprised of their own powers for shaping or influencing the cosmos. In some cases a sort of natural sympathy between human and cosmic behavior seems to be assumed, such that if humans behave correctly and/or rightly focus their minds and wills, the cosmos will respond by providing rain and other effects that humans need to carry on life. There may be a feeling of bidirectional—centripetal and centrifugal—flow of cosmic influence. Human influence on the cosmos in some instances takes the form of rather mechanical magical actions. In other cases, humans can influence the cosmos only through the mediation of the gods; then the question becomes, what are the means through which humans can influence the gods (entreaty? ritual? sacrifice?).

Modern technologies have extended human influence far beyond the level of village life, and it is no wonder that technology has propelled mythlike depictions in modern film and literature. But the immense power of technology to shape human life has always played a part in mythology, and it is interesting to note that, in traditional mythologies, those technologies that greatly influence human life tend to draw gods or other ultimate cosmic forces into the story. Such is of course the case with the many and varied stories of humans gaining control of fire, but also with stories of humans gaining control of other aspects of nature, for example, in the series of cosmic battles with water portrayed in the Babylonian *Enuma Elish*, which provided mythological and ritual backing for a political bureaucracy organized around controlled irrigation. Perhaps it is not just the memorable performances of notable actors, but the topic itself—the battles for control of water that made possible the city of Los Angeles—that has given the film *Chinatown* a kind mythic status in the world of cinema.

Mythologies can play on both proportionality and disproportionality of cause and effect throughout various aspects of a culture. Dante's *Inferno*, the section of his *Divine Comedy* portraying hell, draws a large part of its appeal from the ingenious fitting of punishment to crime, as Dante imaginatively pairs the misdeeds of this world with the penalties for them to be endured in the next. His poetic cosmic vision conveys a sense of control, for we see that we can shape our existence in the afterlife through our behavior in this one. But mythologies can also dramatize a disproportion between cause and effect, and they do so often in portrayals of those aspects of existence that lie beyond our control, such as our mortality. Many mythologies account for the origin of death, and often they do so by referring the necessity of death to the most trivial of causes. A notable example, made famous by the mythologist James Frazer, is the tale of the "perverted message," in which human mortality is said to result from an animal messenger mixing up the message he is sent by a creator to deliver to humanity in the beginning of time. There can be a "founder effect," or a sense that whatever happens early in the unfolding of the cosmos will exert a disproportionate effect on what follows; perhaps this contributes to our human inclination to invest the earliest moments of the cosmos with a heightened sacredness.

Finally, the myriad of forces, motives, actions, and events comprised in a mythology can *together* give rise to and convey a *worldview*: a sense of the overall feel or character of the cosmos and of existence within it. Is the cosmos peaceful or tranquil? Organized or disorganized? Firm and reliable or contingent and full of accidents? Pliable or resistant to tampering? To be taken at face value or full of unpredictable, invisible forces or entities? Can new things be created out of nothing ("**ex nihilo**") by the will of a creator, or only out of preexisting matter? Should we be optimistic or fatalistic? Some mythologies speak directly of such matters; others present colorful stories and leave it the hearers/readers to draw their own inferences.

Relation: points to keep in mind
- motive force(s) by which the cosmos comes to be (e.g., human-like will? sexual desire and procreation? powers inherent in nature and in matter?)
- the moral character (altruistic? evil? indifferent? a mixture?) of forces of cosmogenesis
- kinds and distributions of power and influence (among kinds of beings, genders, regions of cosmos)

- the different kinds of kinship relationships, and the specific forms of connection created or exerted through these
- shifts in power, and how these occur (theft, cleverness, conquest, voluntary bestowal, etc.)
- relation of power and knowledge (perfect knowledge? perfect power? creation *ex nihilo*?)
- proportion or disproportion of cosmic cause and effect
- means by which humans can influence the cosmos (sympathy, magic, entreaty, etc.)
- worldview: overall feel or character of the cosmos and human existence (hostile or friendly? stable or ever-changing? predictable or contingent?)

Conclusion

The axes of comparison set out above, and the points raised under each, are not ends in themselves. Depending on the mythology considered, some points will be more useful than others, and the student may discover points in addition to, and perhaps more important than, those discussed above. Any such grid, and especially its illustrative examples, will be influenced by the expertise and limitations of the grid's designers; and, in the end, no comparative grid will be able to anticipate the complexities and subtleties of all mythologies, let alone of any mythology. To isolate such axes is also of course somewhat artificial, since in the end all five axes fuse in mythological narratives. Finally, the axes of comparison set out above are limited to the *content and structure* of mythic narratives; they do not speak to factors involved in the *actual performance* of myths—the latter will be addressed in the conclusion of chapter 4.

Despite these limitations, however, such axes, and the analytical points raised within each, offer places to begin and pointers that can help students to formulate useful questions, to characterize and compare different mythologies, and, one hopes, to notice patterns and details that would not otherwise have been noticed. Although analytical grids applied inflexibly can constrict our vision, used creatively and flexibly they can prime us to broaden our vision by actively engaging the topics of our study.

As noted at the outset, the values of comparison are several. In briefest terms, comparison helps us to realize and appreciate the diversity and variety of ways in which humans have understood the cosmos and their place in it. Comparison helps us to develop an informed view of possible universals in human nature and culture—over against the uninformed pronouncements one encounters daily on this matter. Comparison of different mythologies can also suggest possible processes and routes through which mythologies have developed, diverged, and converged. Finally, even if one is devoted to one particular mythology, nothing is as useful as comparison in revealing the distinctive or unique qualities of any particular object; and, as a corollary, comparison puts us in position to more clearly see our own mythology.

Sources of Comparative Examples

History of Aryan race theories: Lincoln, *Theorizing Myth* (1999).
Indo-European mythology: Puhvel, *Comparative Mythology* (1987).
Dumézil's Indo-European theories: Littleton, *The New Comparative Mythology* (1982).
Flood myths: Dundes, *The Flood Myth* (1988).
Linear and Cyclical Time: Eliade, *The Myth of the Eternal Return* (2005).
Australian Dream Time: Stanner, "The Dreaming" (1956).
Creation and Transformation: Boas, "The Mythologies of the Indians" (1905–1906).
Hopi Emergence Myth: Courlander, *The Fourth World of the Hopis* (1971); Vecsey, "The Emergence and Maintenance of the Hopi

People," in *Imagine Ourselves Richly* (1991); Zolbrod, *Diné bahane', The Navajo Creation Story* (2010).

Arawakan Wakuénai of Venezuela: Hill, "Made from Bone" (2002).

Polynesian genealogical cosmogony: Beckwith, ed., *The Kumulipo* (1986); Best, *Maori Religion and Mythology*, Part I (1976).

Feats of Polynesian Maui: Grey, *Polynesian Mythology* (1855); Luomala, *Maui-of-a-Thousand-Tricks* (1949).

Earth-diver myths: Rooth, "The Creation Myths of the North American Indians" (1984).

Myths of Sky and Earth as parents: Numazawa, "The Cultural-Historical Background of Myths on the Separation of Sky and Earth" (1984); Belcher, *African Myths of Origins* (2005).

Vertical/horizontal in travel guide: Barthes, "The *Blue Guide*," in *Mythologies* (1995).

Raven and his journey: Boas, *Tsimshian Mythology* (1916).

Paeli people and landscape: Biersack, "The Mount Kare Python and His Gold" (1999).

Ymir myth: Snorri Sturluson, *The Prose Edda* (c. 1220).

Mesocosm: Levy, *Mesocosm* (1991).

Timor, tip, and trunk: Traube, *Cosmology and Social Life* (1986).

Western Apache place-names: Basso, "Speaking with Names" (1989).

Chronotope: Bakhtin, *The Dialogic Imagination* (1982).

Maori god Whakarū: see discussion in Schrempp, *Magical Arrows* (1992), 111–17.

Hopi twins: Courlander, *The Fourth World of the Hopis* (1971); Radin, "The Basic Myth of North American Indians" (1950).

Pacific Island directional system: see, for example, Handy and Handy, *Native Planters in Old Hawaii* (1972).

Irish portal to underworld: see, for example, *Tales of the Elders of Ireland* (Acallam na Senórach) (original c. 1200).

One-and-two: Plato, *Symposium* (1971); Eliade, *The Two and the One* (1969); Hesiod, *Theogony* (1985), with introduction by Norman O. Brown.

Duality and the Dogon: Marcel Griaule, *Conversations with Ogotemmêli: An Introduction to Dogon Religious Ideas* (1970) [1965].
Native American patterns of four: Cushing, "The Cock and the Mouse" (1965).
Aido-Hwedo (the Serpent) and the shaping of the landscape among the Fon: Courlander, *A Treasury of African Folklore: The Oral Literature, Traditions, Myths, Legends, Epics, Tales, Recollections, Wisdom, Sayings, and Humor of Africa* (2002).
Cosmos as inventor's workshop: Cormier, "A Preliminary Review of Neotropical Primates in the Subsistence and Symbolism of Indigenous Lowland South American Peoples" (2006); Dennis Tedlock, *Popol Vuh* (1996).
Cosmic proliferation and reduction: Brown, introduction in Hesiod, *Theogony* (1985); Lévi-Strauss, *The Raw and the Cooked* (1969); Girard, *Things Hidden since the Foundation of the World* (1987).
Yoeme and religious conversion: Shorter, *We Will Dance Our Truth* (2009).
Irish fairies as neither for Heaven nor Hell: Carey, *A Single Ray of the Sun* (1999).
Tikopia and religious conversion: Firth, "The Plasticity of Myth" (1984).
Comparative taxonomy and worldview: Kearney, *World View* (1985); Lakoff, *Women, Fire, and Dangerous Things* (1987); Redfield, *The Little Community* (1989).
Jicarilla Apache world-around race: Opler, *Myths and Tales of the Jicarilla Apache* (1938).
Relation of quality and quantity: Hansen, "Poverty of Cause in Mythological Narrative" (2009).
Maori genealogical taxonomies: Best, Maori *Religion and Mythology*, Part I (1976).
Maori story or origin of species: Grey, *Polynesian Mythology* (1855).
Affinal kinship, distributed power in Native American myth: Thompson, "The Star Husband Tale" (1953); Lévi-Strauss,

The Raw and the Cooked (1969); Schrempp, "Distributed Power" (1998).

Interstitial beings, liminality, unity of opposites: Mary Douglas, *Purity and Danger* (2002); van Gennep, *The Rites of Passage* (1961).

Tricksters: Radin, *The Trickster* (1987); Hynes and Doty, *Mythical Trickster Figures* (1997); Babcock-Abrahams, "'A Tolerated Margin of Mess'" (1975).

Story of perverted message: Frazer, "The Fall of Man," in *Folklore in Old Testament* (1988).

Chapter 4

Some Current Trends

The phrase "myth in everyday life" refers to the many ways that myth impacts the daily lived lives of humans around the world. To study this intersection is to look at the ways in which mythology may be said to influence our languages, cognitive categories, worldviews, rituals, institutions, rules, and the like. Such insights are furthered by ongoing careful, contextual research, particularly noticeable in the fields of anthropology, ethnology, and folkloristics. Ethnographers have looked closely at ongoing cultures and cultural dynamics in the various roles played by mythology around the world, with many new and innovative outlooks, as well as extending and adding detail and nuance to many long-standing traditions of inquiry. Other cultural theorists have also joined the discussions, across a wide range of disciplines. In this section, we will delineate a few of the most promising trends in mythological research, with a recognition that further scholarship will continue to refine many of our outlooks, as well as doubtless introducing new ones. One thing to bear in mind is the insight from our historical analysis, that there is always a relationship between mythology, thoughts about mythology, and the society that tells them. This relationship is a dynamic one, constantly changing and being renegotiated over time.

Popular Culture

One approach is to examine the ways that myth appears in cultural productions: not only the traditional oral narratives, but also in various other ways, including, increasingly, popular culture, the realm of television shows, novels, video games, advertisements, films, and much more. Such approaches emphasize the ongoing dynamic in which myth is both expressed and received, a continual back and forth of social production and reception. These intersections of myth and popular culture are among the most prevalent ways in which (especially unfamiliar) myths are experienced by many people in the world today.

As one increasingly encounters myths and myth-like stories and images in the realm of popular culture, "myth" and related terms are increasingly finding their way into the vocabulary of popular-culture criticism and commentary (for example, "avatar," a word that outside of India previously was known mostly by mythologists, is now commonplace in the English language). One way of categorizing instances of myth in/as popular culture is through what one might term different degrees of obviousness.

1. Most obvious would be recognizable myths, previously passed along orally or in writing, but now promulgated through modern media such as film, television, or comic books. There is a strong strain of the "usual suspects" (e.g., Greek mythology, Norse mythology, Abrahamic mythology), but besides these, world audiences are increasingly tuning into myths from around the world, including ongoing mythic traditions. For example the film *Whale Rider* recounts a Maori origin myth, yet does so in a way that shows the myth as an ongoing part of the culture, a part that is also subject to contemporary influences and changes, such as the rise of global feminism. The very point of this movie seems to be the importance of ongoing indigenous mythologies, not as

remnants of the past, but as adaptable parts of contemporary society.
2. One step less obvious would be productions in which recognizably classic myths are repackaged in modern garb: an ancient story reset in the modern world. An example would be the 1959 film *Black Orpheus* in which the classical Greek story of Orpheus and Eurydice is set in the context of Carnival in modern Rio de Janeiro.
3. A further degree of removal from the obvious occurs in modern creations inspired not by any specific story, but rather by a generic myth-plot formula abstracted from ancient stories. The best-known example of course would be George Lucas's reliance on the generic hero-story plot summary put forward in Joseph Campbell's *Hero with a Thousand Faces* as the framework for the *Star Wars* movies.
4. Still another step less obvious would be contemporary creations that appeal neither to any particular ancient myth nor to a generic plot-formula, but merely to something like a generic mythic/legend world. This sort of grab is typically made through characters with various sorts of "superpowers" and through tokens—dress, ornament, amulets, landscapes—that convey a sense of the ancient, the supernatural, the cosmic, the mysterious, the magical—in other words, a mixed brew that has something vaguely mythological about it. This form of mythologizing is especially common in film, television, and video games. This can include "alternate universes" that have their own gods and mythologies, sometimes with implicit or even explicit reference to real-world mythologies. For example, J. R. R. Tolkien created a fantasy world for his book series (*Lord of the Rings, The Hobbit*, etc.), but did so by borrowing from various European mythologies (Tolkien was a professor of folklore at Cambridge). Tolkien's work is especially notable, as he set out to make a "fictional mythology" for England,

with heavy doses of both Celtic and Nordic material. Not only was this a remarkable publishing success in its own right, but it also spawned a whole related "swords and sorcery" genre of fiction, an appropriately generative act for purposefully mythic fiction writing.

Barthes's Mythologies of the Bourgeoisie

One of the most important works on popular culture *as* mythology—and perhaps the only "classic" thus far produced on this topic—has only a limited relationship to any of the foregoing categories. Specifically, the extraordinary literary and cultural critic Roland Barthes, in a series of vignettes written in the 1950s, approached the most prosaic elements of French and American popular culture as *Mythologies* (followed by *Eiffel Tower*). His connecting of such prosaic items of middle-class life to myth is, for the most part, less obvious and more subtle than any of the four kinds of connections summarized above, and for that reason is all the more interesting.

For example, in the vignette "The Writer on Holiday," Barthes calls attention to the fact that when photographs of famous writers on vacation appear in popular magazines, such writers are invariably preoccupied and disheveled. Why? Barthes suggests that such portrayals are a journalistic ploy evoking and promoting the mythic status of the writer. Vacation is a phenomenon of human time in which, the photos tell us, writers cannot participate comfortably, for they cannot really take a break. For great writers are vessels of a power of genius beyond the human, for whose summons they must remain perpetually on call.

Another of Barthes's vignettes, "Blue Blood Cruise," is also about a favorite photojournalistic topic, this time, the love of catching members of European royalty acting ordinary—royal men in short-sleeved shirts and women in cotton print dresses. The question Barthes asks is whether such moments really result in this special class of humans becoming ordinary, or whether they amount to a form of "inoculation"—a small bit of contamination introduced to insure the ultimate separateness of two realms. A similar case in American culture might be the tabloid fascination with Hollywood celebrities caught in unkempt everyday moments. Do these moments undo the special status of celebrities? Do we want them to be like us, or does their place in our lives and consciousness derive from their maintaining of a realm that, like that of mythological gods, is parallel to ours more than the same as ours?

Through these and many other vignettes in the first part of *Mythologies*, Barthes cleverly explores subtly mythic elements in a range of phenomena of popular culture including wrestling matches, travel guides, popular magazines, and national cuisines, to mention only the witty, charming, and insightful; but several of these vignettes, especially those relating to politics, are caustic. Moreover, the vignettes are followed, in the second part of *Mythologies*, by a now-famous essay entitled "Myth Today," in which it becomes clear that what Barthes means by myth is middle-class self-delusion. His strongest barb is for middle-class French citizens whose comfortable self-delusions about France's "natural" right to the central place in the world has justified colonialist rule. In Barthes's analyses, the concept of "myth" is not far from the Marxist concepts of "mystification" and "false consciousness," both of which point to the ways in which societies invent ideologies to justify and camouflage political and economic exploitation. Barthes's notion of myth is also related to the term as it is sometimes used by political scientists and commentators to mean something like "propaganda," except that the latter often implies dissemination from a governmental agency, while Barthes sees the middle class as happily contributing to the creation of mythology.

Barthes's critique of colonialism, and the middle class myths that facilitate it, is trenchant and necessary. Still, it must be asked whether all of the topics explored in his opening vignettes rise to the level of perniciousness comprised in colonialism. Consider again Barthes's take on the writer on holiday. Yes, society is complicit in the mythic formulation of the writer as mouthpiece of the Muses, but this bit of heroizing and self-infatuation is also part of what energizes the psyche of the artist as well as the audience's enjoyment and support of the arts. Might not a world lacking in all such conceits be devoid of character and energy; indeed, taken to an extreme might not the ruling out of such imaginative flights be tantamount to the abolition of culture? The term myth has for some time carried a morally ambiguous character: negatively it means "delusion," positively a society's poetic imagining of itself. Unfortunately, the point at which one passes from one to the other is not always easy to locate.

Barthes's vignettes raise yet another issue, one that is implied but not explicit in his analysis, namely: how significant is the quality of ancientness to the concept of myth? For in Barthes's hands, even the most modern images subtly exude ancientness. In "The Face of Garbo," the mesmerizing appeal of this actress is attributed to her eternal, archetypal countenance. In "The Brain of Einstein," Barthes points out that the great physicist allowed his brain to be wired up for scientific study, and that for the general public, uncomprehending of Einstein's theories, the brain as physical object held an appeal like that of the magic amulet in a prescientific worldview. In "Soap-powders and Detergents," Barthes deals with advertisements for the quintessentially modern, middle-class phenomenon of household cleaners; but he does so in a way that might evoke for the reader the ancient four-element theory. That is, Barthes groups ads into three kinds: those that appeal to solvency, foaming action, and abrasion, the last of which, he points out, is typically is linked to imagery of fire. Thus we have water, air, and fire, with dirt (earth) as their object. To those who would resist the idea that modern phenomena can be mythology, Barthes, in such examples, holds out the possibility that the distinction between the ancient and the modern may not always be clear, or in other words, that the modern may also be the ancient.

Barthes's influence can be felt in the works of numerous modern scholars. Marina Warner, for example, writes on the intersection of myth with other genres, such as fairy tales, fiction, and proverbs. For Warner, myths are both ancient and contemporary, continually re-invoked in all aspects of culture. This once again underlines the notion that myths are theoretically hard to pin down, in part because of their extreme ubiquity: as they form a basis for so much of our culture, they continue to be manifested throughout all sorts of cultural expressions. Many current writers on mythology have become increasingly interested in the ongoing use of myth in our daily lives, from video games and advertising to literature and popular science. For example, Candace Slater (2002) has investigated how the Brazilian rainforest reveals a collision of myths: there is the "Edenic view" of the rainforest put forth in advertising commercials, which contrasts to the local, indigenous mythologies and the realities on the ground, with at times tragic results. Collisions of mythologies are always a compelling phenomenon, revealing in this example the assumptions and effects of colonialism and capitalism, and the endangered local indigenous mythic traditions.

New Takes on Myth and History—or, What Really Happened?

A wholly different approach to the possibility of mythology reinvigorates a very old tradition with new scientific data and approaches. The question of whether the events recounted in myths and legends actually happened played a part in the theoretical discourse about myth as far back as Classical Greek and Roman civilization. For example, the question of whether there actually ever was an Atlantis lies behind Plato's dialogue *Critias*, and the story of Atlantis has persisted up to the present. We earlier called attention to the concept of "euhemerism," the theory about the origin of myths proffered by the fourth-century BCE Greek thinker Euhemerus. Euhemerus argued that myths were created as embellished portrayals of actual history and events; thus, according to Euhemerus, myths do reflect actual history though in an exaggerated way. The fifth-century BCE Athenian historian Thucydides adumbrated the issue by championing a new method of writing history—one based on rigorously verified sources, rather than hearsay narratives that he saw his compatriots as typically relying upon.

Perhaps influenced by Thucydides, the first-century BCE Roman historian Livy opened his monumental history of Rome with the question of what sort of stock we should put in the miraculous-seeming stories, such as that of Romulus and Remus, that we have received from tradition. Livy decided to include such stories in his history, less out of conviction of their historical veracity than because they offered important moral lessons that citizens needed to hear in what he regarded as a time of moral decline:

> Events before Rome was born or thought of have come to us in old tales with more of the charm of poetry than of a sound historical record, and such traditions I propose neither to affirm nor refute. There is no reason, I feel, to object when antiquity draws no hard line between the human and the supernatural: it adds dignity to the past, and, if any nation deserves the privilege of claiming a divine ancestry, that nation is our own; and so great is the glory won by the Roman people in their wars that, when they declare that Mars himself was their first parent and father of the man who founded their city, all the nations of the world might well allow the claims as readily as they accept Rome's imperial dominion. (1985, 33–34)

By means of a hedge, then, Livy manages to open his methodical history of Rome with a myth of divine origin.

Somewhat similarly, Snorri Sturluson (1179–1241), the Icelandic writer from whom a great deal of our understanding of Norse mythology derives, claimed Odin was a real man, as were all the other gods. The Aesir gods, believed Snorri, came from the East. Thus Snorri, a Christian writer, was able to document a great deal of pagan mythic stories under the guise of ancient history.

And as we have seen, in England, the effectiveness of mythology as a record of what actually happened was a topic of great interest: many scholars in the nineteenth century believed Arthur was a real king. David MacRitchie (1851–1925) further proposed that the Celtic supernatural others of brownies, pixies, and so on were folk memories of an earlier, pygmy race. Such topics were hotly debated in the realm of folklore studies during its most formative period in the nineteenth century.

During the twentieth century, however, discovering true history behind mythic narratives was accorded less attention than questions concerning what such narratives can tell us about our nature as humans, how societies and our minds work, and moral issues such as the meaning of good and evil. Such questions hearken back to the allegorical tradition launched by Classical Greek thinkers, and carried out through the Middle Ages and Renaissance, that myths should not be read at face value but as containing a hidden, poetic truth. The most dominant myth theories of the twentieth century similarly were less concerned with "what actually happened" than with what mythic narratives tell us about human nature, psychology, and society. The sociological "functionalist" schools of Durkheim and Malinowski were concerned with the roles played by myths in maintaining society and individuals within those societies. Myths provide symbols that promote positive social behavior; they explain how rituals originated, and thus validate them; they lay out the basic rules and design of a society; they provide role models and thus paths of maturation for members of society. None of this demands that myths reflect actual historical events.

A particularly revealing example of the privileging of social function of myth over the question of historical factuality is offered by George Dumézil's analysis of the "Rape of the Sabine," a famous story that recounts how the early inhabitants of Rome, facing a shortage of women, invited their neighbors, the Sabines, to view the new city, then seized the Sabine women for wives. Dumézil, though a scholar of Indo-European languages, was greatly influenced by

Durkheim's sociological theories; and in analyzing the story of the Sabine, Dumézil largely dismisses prehistorical evidence that might be taken as support that the event actually occurred, in favor of an interpretation that emphasizes the social symbols that the story displays. Specifically, Dumézil argues that the story is a dramatization of the origin of Roman civilization through a combining of the three functions that, he claims, make up the Indo-European model of the well-formed society. The Romans possessed the first and second functions, a system of rule and military prowess, while the opulent Sabines stood for the missing third "function": fertility and agriculturalism. Dumézil likens the Roman story to a story found in another Indo-European society, one quite distant from Rome, specifically the Norse story of the intermarriage of the Aesir and Vanir gods, who, Dumézil claims, similarly embody the complementary qualities possessed by the Latins and the Sabines. Dumézil's analysis of the Rape of the Sabine forms part of a larger claim by Dumézil that events depicted in other Indo-European myths often are recast in Rome as historical legends.

Dumézil's analysis epitomizes an approach to myth maximally invested in what myth tells us about the nature of society, in particular Indo-European notions about how society should be structured, and minimally invested in whether the events recounted ever actually happened. Something similar can be said for most major myth theorists of the twentieth century. Psychoanalytic theories saw myths as mechanisms of managing and transcending unavoidable conflicts between the instinctual and social realms. Joseph Campbell says that myth should be read as psychology, and that one who reads it as biography, history, or cosmology is misreading it (2004, 237). Even though he emphasized the concept of "sacred history," Mircea Eliade with this concept was less concerned with whether specific events recounted actually occurred than with the way that temporally distant moments served as foci for sacred rituals. Claude Lévi-Strauss's prolific and inspired writings on mythology had many influences, including Durkheim and Freud; for Lévi-Strauss, as for his intellectual ancestors, myth was about the mind ruminating on the dilemmas of existence more than on whether the scenarios through which such dilemmas are explored ever actually happened.

What if events in myths *did* actually happen? Would it matter?

Perhaps not: consider that many important events that did occur did *not* become myths. If myths relate what happened, they may do so in a different way and in a different spirit than the history written by academic historians. While the latter normally seek to discover "what really happened," myths create a powerful story, taking what happened and imbuing it with meaning. In the end, the symbolic aspects become the focus, rather than the events themselves.

Or, perhaps it would matter: consider that epochal, important events in a culture would likely be remembered, and interpreted in a culturally meaningful way. Thus, earthquakes and tsunamis could be remembered by the Northwest Coast groups as caused by "Mountain Dwarfs Dancing" (MacMillan and Hutchinson 2002), a motif engaged in various social and cultural functions (for instance, most often the Mountain Dwarfs dance due to someone breaking a taboo). Yet also we may observe the ways in which the story recapitulates the long-term occurrences of earthquakes and tsunamis in a way that makes it real and compelling for people who have never personally experienced such a thing (yet may well, some day). The story also decisively links earthquakes with tsunamis, imparting important information. Included in many of the stories are the ways in which some people survived, while other people perished. Thus, the real-world existence of earthquakes and tsunamis is an ongoing concern for many Northwest Coast groups, and acknowledging the relationship between what did happen (earthquakes) and the mythologies may be important on many levels.

If the issue of what myths tell us about "what actually happened" was not a dominant issue in twentieth-century myth theory, recent decades have seen several strands of re-emerging interest in this issue. Particularly influential has been a series of carefully researched publications by Adrienne Mayor that have presented evidence supporting a factual basis for many different myths, such as amazons and griffins. We could also note the continuing work in Ireland that lines up oral traditions with archaeological findings: for example, the Corlea Trackway is a massive oaken road unearthed by Barry Raftery, which was convincingly connected to the remarks in the ancient Irish story *Tochmarc Étaíne* ("The Wooing of Étaín"), through dendrochronology and carbon analysis on the one hand, and historical and literary research of the ancient Irish texts on the other. In this case, the text, written over a thousand years ago, had recorded an oral tale from almost a thousand years still earlier; the story looked just as fantastic as many others, until the trackway itself was unearthed, examined, and dated to 148–147 BCE, lining up in the annals to the correct date mentioned in the story.

This strand of research interest has grown particularly in regards to indigenous traditions, and especially around instances in which mythical stories converge with geology, archaeology, genetics, and other "strong-science" disciplines. In her groundbreaking book *Legends of the Earth* (1973), Dorothy Vitaliano, who coined the term "**geomythology**," notes many such convergences, from colorful etiological stories about local land formations to Plato's account of Atlantis. One focus of her discussion is stories that reflect volcanic activity. An example that has come to be much discussed concerns a story told by the Klamath Indians of the Northwest area of the United States, in which, from two mountain peaks, Chiefs of the Below World and Above World battled each other until the mountain of the Chief of the Below World, Mount Mazama, collapsed, leaving a hole from which Crater Lake was formed. Vitaliano says, "The interesting thing about this legend is that, stripped of the supernatural elements, it describes rather accurately how Crater Lake *was* formed. Mount Mazama did erupt with great violence and collapse more than 6,500 years ago, leaving the depression now occupied by the lake" (1973, 123).

In *Red Earth, White Lies: Native Americans and the Myth of Scientific Fact* (1995), Native American writer Vine Deloria Jr.

cites Vitaliano's analysis of the Klamath story of Crater Lake, along with many other Native American stories about the landscape, in a thought-provoking comparison of knowledge as propounded in traditional narratives and in Western science. He argues that Western science has achieved an authority that leads to a glossing over of its defects, including frequent partialness of data, a quickness to fall into orthodoxies, and a sense of infallibility. At the same time a variety of prejudices has worked against according anything like an equal status to Native American oral traditions. One prejudice is the racist assumption that white men are methodical and objective while Native Americans are unreliable and superstitious. Another is that for Native Americans,

> oral traditions refer *only* to religious matters. This description is not true. The bulk of American Indian traditions probably deal with commonsense ordinary topics such as plants, animals, weather, and past events that are not particularly of a religious nature. (1995, 51)

Deloria emphasizes especially that motives of personal gain operating in the Western scientific establishment, and the skewing of knowledge to which these can lead, are not prevalent in the social context of Native American oral traditions. Deloria's book is a thoughtful and provocative look at social attitudes toward two forms of knowledge by an individual whose life encompasses both.

In their work *When They Severed Earth from Sky*, Elizabeth and Paul Barber also discuss the Klamath story of Crater Lake, as well as many other instances of geology-recounting myths, with a strong emphasis on ways in which myths process and store environmental information, including warnings about environmental hazards such as volcanic eruptions, in a form that will be efficient, memorable, and useful for future generations. Drawing upon cognitive science, they formulate specific principles summarizing "how the human mind shapes myth" (their book's subtitle) to such ends. For example, a principle they term the "redundancy strategy" says that "because of the importance attached, particular information will tend to be encoded with a high degree of redundancy and/or vividness, *except* where the piece of knowledge is believed to be universal" (2004, 245). The "kinship principle" says: "if two (willful) phenomena are perceived as alike, they must be kinsfolk. (Scientists say, like effects imply like causes; but myths say, like effects imply kinship between the willful beings)" (2004, 245). These are but two examples from a detailed list intended to describe the cognitive processes involved in the creation of orally transmitted myths that, they claim, exist largely to encode useful information about the environment.

Similarly, a reevaluation of Australian mythologies has repeatedly emphasized incidences of confluence between the mythic stories and scientific knowledge, particularly in the realm of geology. As noted before, Australian mythology is keenly focused on the formation of the landscape. With mythic traditions stretching back in place over 60,000 years, Australia represents a perhaps unique place in the world to view such long-term recordings of environmental change and geological activity. Such re-evaluations may help lend appreciation and understanding of embattled Aboriginal societies, languages, and cultures, as well as help such groups claim for a recognition of their traditions, and an end to ongoing colonialist belittlement of their stories and spirituality as "primitive" or "savage." It may even help them regain more control of the various territories they have inhabited for tens of thousands of years.

The impact of colonial thinking is increasingly recognized, and the way that the denial of veracity of oral traditions has long been used as a tool to delegitimize indigenous owners of land, and to make claims for colonial invaders. Western discourse has conveniently denied the historical legitimacy of various groups via the denial of the veracity of oral traditions. All this has led to a reconsideration in many parts of the world of the impact of colonial thought about myths for various, especially indigenous, peoples. The question of the relationship between mythology and the actual past has become a great focus of concern for many groups, often with legal implications, especially regarding land rights. Indigenous peoples often find their stories represented in colonialist caricatures, and their own interpretive traditions not given voice in colonial discourses.

One problem is that taking mythology as a guide to the actual past can lead to extremely speculative reconstructions. For example, Marinus van der Sluijs and Anthony L. Peratt combine a detailed survey of the geographical distribution of the mythical image of the ouroboros—a snake, worm, or dragon swallowing its own tail—with findings of historical plasma physics and astronomy. They argue that the condition of Earth's atmosphere in the late Neolithic was quite different from that of today, and may have produced more intense and encompassing aurorae than we now observe. They speculate that these may be the inspiration for the ouroboros image. Linking their project to that of geomythology, they say:

> Within the history of ideas, the hypothesis that the worldwide motif of the tail-biting dragon was originally based on observations of an extreme type of aurora fits into recently revived scholarly interests in transient natural phenomena as the ultimate inspiration for widespread mythical themes. (2009, 27)

Does this sort of speculation mark a bold new interdisciplinary venture made possible by modern science, or a return to the unbridled extravagance of nineteenth-century "solar mythology"?

Diachronic Analyses

Another way in which the reflection of historical facts in myth can be approached is through attention to the ways that mythologies change through time, in what is called "diachronic" analyses. Such studies give nuance to the ongoing dynamic of mythologies as cultural performances, showing how all traditions, even the most conservative, change over time, and how these changes reflect and adapt to changes in the worlds of the people performing them.

One of the most significant and wide-reaching events, whose effects are registered in mythologies throughout the world, is the expansion of European peoples from the sixteenth century onward, a movement that often took the form of colonialist expansion and the perpetration of new beliefs with missionaries. Many examples can be cited. A particularly interesting example is furnished by the anthropologist Raymond Firth (1984), who noticed two elements in Tikopian mythology that, at the time he encountered the Tikopians in 1929, most probably were recent innovations, one more illustrative of new technology introduced by Europeans—specifically iron with its superior hardness—the other illustrative of conflicts between old and new religious beliefs. Regarding the first, Firth encountered a story about the origin of a temple that, he concludes, incorporates concerns that significantly postdate the time in which the temple was most likely built. Specifically, the story tells why the white men had iron while the Tikopians lacked this substance until the white men brought it. The story tells of the temple being built by sibling gods. When the senior-sibling god asked his juniors to hand him iron nails, they only gave him coconut sinnet cord; so when the temple was completed, the senior god took the nails to the land of the white men.

The second change involves religious beliefs, and takes the form not of an addition to a narrative scenario, but rather of the growth of a new type of story. Specifically, Tikopians recounted that the missionaries, in an attempt to induce the Tikopians to convert to Christianity, threw a stone sacred to indigenous beliefs into the ocean; but of its own power the stone returned to its rightful location and in other ways defied attempts to do away with its power. Eventually, in a sort of tacit compromise, the Tikopians agreed to convert to Christianity, but a whole new set of stories about the stone grew up as though to ensure that the old powers of Tikopia would not be disrespected by new religious practitioners, who, according to Firth, were not beyond treating the new stories with some deference.

Whatever "really happened" with regard to the specifics of the temple and the stone, such mythical innovations, which can be found all over the world, attest to historical reality in deep and powerful ways: first, they testify to the basic situation of confrontations between different cultures, technologies, and religious beliefs, often in situations of unequal power; and secondly, they testify, in a way that no record created from an outsider's perspective can, to the meanings that the confrontations had for those who create the mythological innovations.

Another revealing example can be seen in the Navajo "Blessingway" chant, a mythological recitation of the emergence into the area of people and animals. Barre Toelken noted how one chanter included sheep in the mythological poem, although it was common knowledge that the sheep had been introduced by the Spanish. Yes, his informant related, we all know that, but the sheep is important to us as a people, and therefore it should be represented in the mythological creation story. In this case, a specific innovation was knowingly reworked into the mythic narrative, giving it place and meaning in the Navajo cultural world, following the real-world importance of sheep in Navajo society (Toelken 2002).

Resolving, yet Sustaining, the Dichotomy

New researches have revealed some astounding examples of cultural memories being kept alive in myths for thousands of years, challenging the notion that myths are always best viewed as "untrue" renditions of what actually happened. We can note that epochal impacts (tidal waves, meteorites, invasions, etc.) can often become important stories for cultures in times of changes and new beginnings, and can be retained by these cultures, being reinterpreted and integrated into the wider cultural-mythic fabric. At the same time, it is also widely acknowledged that myths are not always or necessarily good guides to actual events. The tension between what may have happened, and mythic stories, is an ongoing one, due perhaps to different ways of regarding the relationship between perceived reality, storytelling, and the construction of meaning. Researches into these questions are always fraught, and the most convincing studies have been those with a deep contextual view of the tradition, as well as bringing in other realms of inquiry, such as geology, astronomy, archaeology, history, and genetics—all of which can contribute, but none of which is infallible or beyond the possibility of bias.

Heritage

Another way of thinking about the relationship of myths and the past is in terms of heritage. Whereas traditions are always ongoing, and always changing, the concept of heritage implies a bit of the opposite, that one's own identity can be intrinsically linked with practices from the past. In this formulation, the past becomes a resource for identity construction, both on the individual and community levels. How do mythic traditions help people build and maintain cultural cohesion and identity, particularly in this rapidly changing and globalizing world?

The concept of heritage supplies answers for many people. Cultural heritage is the general proposition of a proprietary relationship between individuals and past cultural beliefs, practices, and traditions. Heritage builds from the root ideas of *inheriting*, to be an *heir*, and in this way puts forth the position that some individuals have inherited certain rights and/or privileges regarding past cultural practices. Anyone could, potentially, participate in a tradition, but not everyone can participate in heritage. Heritage is thus a way of creating corporate groups from the inclusion of some individuals and the exclusion of others. Unsurprisingly, heritage can become contentious, as various individuals and groups can make competing claims. For example, the Temple Mount is one of the most holy sites in Judaism, as it was here that King Solomon was said to have built his temple housing the Ark of the Covenant. Problematically, it is also one of the most sacred sites for Islam, since it was also here that Mohammed was said to have ascended to heaven. To whom does this site—or rather the stories regarding the site, and the rights to worship there—belong? This particular locale has been a flashpoint, and the sparks from such contested heritage have led to several *intifadas*, assassinations, murders, military actions, and many, many deaths.

Heritage can also be problematic in that (unlike tradition), it is *assumed* to exist, rather than being objectively observable. Heritage does not *occur*, but is rather a *claim* of a proprietary relationship toward cultural practices. The "heritage model" of culture, including mythology, has received a great deal of public, governmental, and scholarly attention. In trying to delineate such proprietary relationships between individuals and mythology, various social and legal factors become involved, including macro-governmental institutions such as nation-states and global organizations such as UNESCO and various projects of the United Nations. After all, if mythology is heritage, then there is an assumed legal ownership of the myths implied in this formulation. The most central question invoked in the heritage model is: to whom does myth belong?

The idea of some group *owning* myth may seem antithetical to many strands of Western thought. Abrahamic traditions, the dominant discourse, tend to be proselytizing religions, preaching a universal god and mythology for all people. The strongly held notion of "freedom of religion" in Western discourse necessarily implies a belief in the freedom for any individual to take on the belief in any religious strand of thought, including its mythological aspects. The idea of mythology as private property seems strange and foreign.

Yet, many indigenous groups think exactly the opposite: that their traditions are *theirs*, and ultimately up to them to decide how to perform, represent, or even relate to others. These attitudes are doubtless heightened by the tragic history of colonial oppression against indigenous peoples, their cultures, religions, and ways of life. Indigenous groups have increasingly advocated for more ownership of their own cultures and traditions, including their mythology. For example, when some of the most sacred symbols of the Zia Pueblo appeared, trademarked, as a part of a company's portable toilets, the group was outraged. For them this was further illustration of ongoing colonial attitudes of degradation of their most sacred beliefs (see, e.g., Turner 2012). The profitable marketing of indigenous mythology around the world by non-indigenous entrepreneurs has deepened this ideological split.

The Pueblo groups provide many leading examples of this trend. For Pueblo groups, their myths can only rightly be performed by specifically designated persons. Even within Pueblo society, the right to perform different myths belongs to different groups, creating a complex system of interlocking parts that is safeguarded in part by rigorous control over the performances.

Scholarship is not exempt: in 2016 the Acoma Pueblo denounced as "theft" a scholarly book on their mythology, crafted by an eminent Native Studies scholar from publicly available materials (see Lozada 2016). For the Acoma, the provenance of the material for the anthropologist didn't matter: what did matter was that the performance rights of the myth, which belonged squarely within the Acoma—and, even more specifically, among various specific groups within Acoma society. For them, the publication of a book of their mythology by an outsider should be considered the same as trafficking in stolen goods.

The line between legality and ethics is a fluid one: the idea of "appropriations" of culture can be discussed in terms of ethics, legality, or both. When is "appropriation" the same as "intercultural learning" and when is it different? Concerns regarding appropriations include musical genres (gnawa and gnawa-pop), instruments (Native American flute, Australian dijiridu), medical knowledge, sacred teachings, and just about any aspect of human culture (for further discussion, see Michael Brown's 2003 *Who*

Owns Native Culture?). Appropriation can be viewed as the employment of other people's cultural traditions in a way that does not give sufficient credit and value to the origins and the original authors and performers of the traditions, or in ways that they would consider objectionable. Inter-cultural learning, often involving the same material, can be seen, by contrast, as a way of using the material to learn respectfully about the other cultures, and traditions. The territory separating these two terms, and their appropriate boundaries, are, of course, constantly up for interpretations and contestations, and particularly in the realm of the sacred.

The question "who owns myth?" is, thus, a complex and contested one, both legally and ethically, and influences how our increasingly globalized society will continue to participate in mythic traditions in times to come.

Sustainability

Another current trend may be highlighted by the word "sustainability," and involve other well-known phrases such as "decolonization," "language revivals," "traditional ecological knowledge," "indigenous rights," and the like. Increasingly, minority and especially indigenous groups have been asserting their rights to their own culture, including such major elements as language, religion, and way of life. These struggles have moved from the arena of indigenous vs. nation-state to the global stage, as indigenous peoples have been increasingly able to voice their concerns to a global audience. Indigenous groups in the world today represent a major source of diversity in terms of culture, yet are often under pressure from state institutions, and peoples, to abandon their traditions and mythology in favor of the more dominant ones.

In the past, dealings with indigenous groups were often conducted through the distorting lens of racism and ethnic supremacy. Increasingly, scholars have come to appreciate the vast wealth of knowledge of indigenous groups, particularly in regards to their own natural environment. Such information is not always in a form readily available to the academic researcher: For example, the quickly growing idea of TEK, or *traditional ecological knowledge*, is often both descriptive and spiritual, eschewing the boundaries held by Western traditions. The idea of animism, that animals and plants have souls and thus need to be respected, forms the basis of many indigenous mythologies, and is reflected in overall concerns of ethics between the human and the non-human world. The qualities stressed in such myths are those of symbiosis and respectful relationships with nature.

A look at the various salmon cultures of the Pacific Northwest, for example, reveals various ways that the views of salmon have been informed by mythology, influencing the proper ways people interact with them. Widespread stories include the general notion of human responsibility ensuring that the salmon are successful in their grand cycles of spawning, seafaring, and returning: over-harvesting is forbidden, and care given to spawning beds. As Cullon put it, regarding the Kwakwaka'wakw, "These animist beliefs resulted in the care and maintenance of the resource and a sensitivity to salmon ecology that resulted in effective stewardship techniques and an abundance of fish" (2010: 21). This is not just relegated to salmon, but rather is indicative of the overall worldview of many indigenous groups regarding the natural world, a relationship established and sustained by their mythologies. Recent anthropological works aimed at understanding such worldviews include Julie Cruikshank's *Do Glaciers Listen?* and Eduardo Kohn's *How Forests Think*. Such titles reflect the puzzling, if overdue, engagement between Western and indigenous views.

It is interesting to note, for example, how Inuit groups, who are already dealing with some of the more devastating effects of global climate change, have often referred to these changes through their traditional mythological lens: for Inuit, Sedna was a divinity of the underworld (and particularly under the ocean) and responsible for the animals and plants, while Sila is a divine personification of weather and climate. Both deities could become unpleasant when disrespected, which for many Inuit harmonizes well with the ongoing environmental and cultural devastation. To restore balance, the discourse suggests, one must first and foremost restore respectful attitudes and deeds (see, e.g., Leduc, 2010).

The idea of ecological sustainability, of not overusing one's environment, has become attractive to many non-indigenous as well, as the developed world is increasingly facing the dire environmental consequences of its own worldview. Mythologies, then, may hold some keys to understanding how to live sustainably, and may hold some of the keys for our future survival, however difficult that may yet prove to be.

It is not only ecological knowledge that mythologies can both store and sustain, but other kinds of knowledge as well. Some of the most compelling research in this area examines the fundamental categories that myths provide, ideally in a reflective sense, with an awareness that there are vastly different ways of imagining the world, and that our own categories are shaped at least in part by our culture, as well. Recent philosophical research into the areas of posthumanism (which problematizes our category of "the human"), for example, can learn from other traditions where this categorical divide between "humans" and "animals" is not so apparent, as in the many Native American myths where the lines between animal and human are remarkably fluid. This can be contrasted to the politically dominant Abrahamic origin story, in which a humanlike deity creates the world especially for humankind, with the rest of the world being created solely as the dominion of humans. Likewise, while Abrahamic discourses position the earth itself as non-divine and mundane, many cosmologies take the opposite approach—such as the Australian Dreamtime, which give primacy and sacred meaning to the creation of the landscape itself. Unsurprisingly, differences in mythic views can result in clashes over political positions in such matters as mining, development, pollution, and resource management.

Many times such categorical constructions are also reflected in languages. The wide diversity of human languages is quickly disappearing, and our present academic knowledge about languages has vastly increased due to often dwindling and endangered indigenous languages. Like mythologies (and often linked to them), languages are often under sustained pressure in the face of those of the dominant colonial societies. For many indigenous groups around the world, the issues of language, environment, mythology, and culture are fused with their ongoing struggles of political and economic recognition, and a future for their culture, and for the environment.

Mythology, as a central aspect of culture, can become a unifying symbol of social and cultural cohesion, survival, and renaissance. In many cases, indigenous groups have been able to use their mythic traditions to continue to survive, and to continue sustainable livelihoods. In Canada, the Sahtuto'ine of northern Canada successfully argued for the territory of over 36,000 square miles, surrounding the Great Bear Lake, to be declared a UNESCO Biosphere Reserve, a category limiting further development in the area, and granting the Sahtuto'ine sovereignty over the territory. At the time of this writing, another case is with the Canadian Supreme Court, having for over twenty years pitted prospective developers of the Jumbo Ski Resort against the Ktunaxa nation, for whom the remote area is known as Qat'muk, the place of their creation story, and the ongoing home of the great Grizzly Bear Spirit. If in the past, indigenous religious concerns were rarely given consideration, there are signs that that may be changing. In 2007, the United Nations Declaration on the Rights of Indigenous Peoples (signed by 148 states) stated that "Indigenous peoples have the right to manifest, practice, develop and teach their spiritual and religious traditions, customs and ceremonies" (UN General Assembly 2007: 6) and that "Indigenous peoples have the right to maintain and strengthen their distinctive spiritual relationship with their traditionally owned or otherwise occupied and used lands, territories, waters and coastal seas and other resources and to uphold their responsibilities to future generations in this regard" (10).

Contemporary/New/Emergent Mythologies

Revitalizations and new directions in mythologies are not restricted to the indigenous. Researchers have also paid attention to other ongoing mythic traditions, revitalized traditions, and new traditions as well. The awareness of how to recognize mythology, and the impact of mythology in one's own life, allows for a reflective view on many contemporary mythic traditions throughout the world.

The Abrahamic traditions of Judaism, Christianity, and Islam all share one central ancestor figure, "Father Abraham," one deity, the "Father God," and one cosmogonic tradition and overall cosmogony. All share the origin story of the Garden of Eden. Abrahamic religions are currently the most widespread of all mythic traditions, held by a large percentage of the world's population, and influencing a good deal more. Investigations into the various Abrahamic traditions continues from a variety of religious and area studies, and continues to supply new material helping to inform mythological research. In many parts of the world, and in many mythic traditions, it is impossible to ignore the influences of Abrahamic mythology, and teachings, on other mythic traditions. Combined with the impact of colonialism under European colonization, the impact of Abrahamic mythologies on many other mythologies cannot be overstated. As Abrahamic mythology has spread around the globe to multitudes of different cultures and peoples, it has continued to be rethought, and reinterpreted, in different areas and among different groups.

Most nation-states in the world are avowedly Abrahamic in institutional affiliation, and many others are unofficially so. Other state-supported mythic traditions are few in number, but include a substantial number of the world's population. In India, Hinduism and other Vedic traditions continue to predominate. Buddhism provides other mythic traditions for other areas. Japan also acknowledges Shintoism, while Mongolia recognizes Shamanism. Many folk mythological traditions continue in China, in spite of official state rejection of religion.

Besides long-standing mythic traditions are also new traditions, and revitalized older ones. As covered in the history section, and somewhat in opposition to the androcentric Abrahamic traditions, various "goddess" movements, including most famously Wicca, have emerged and continued to gain membership in a highly re-crafted tradition. Wicca, and the imagining of the earth as a personified goddess deity, draws many ecologically concerned people together with various mythic traditions, ranging from indigenous to European. Concern regarding the environment plays a central role in many of these oppositional discourses, with links to such other ideologies as feminism and sustainability. While we have previously discussed the use of indigenous traditions, the re-crafting of non-Christian European mythologies is an interesting phenomenon, as well: to what degree do these neo-pagan mythologies intersect with the daily lives of their participants? In what ways are these aligned with the burgeoning belief in heritage? How and why have some of these mythic shifts occurred? Researching contemporary phenomena gives the researcher the opportunity to ask new questions, and to seek detailed data and analyses to help in answering them.

And, finally, contemporary researchers may also take note of new and emergent mythological traditions. One candidate for such a position would be the general, popular notion of extraterrestrial aliens, particularly in those accounts in which such beings play a formative role in human culture, biology, or other formative aspects of our being. While generally considered a relatively new category, it should be noted that this at times synchronizes with earlier, perhaps particularly Abrahamic, mythology.

The idea of "ancient aliens" having a hand in establishing life on earth, or humans, or human civilizations, reveals the use of aliens in the most basic mythic sense of origin stories. Aliens are an increasingly popular way to narrate or imagine our beginnings, and, hence, our categorical ontology—who we *are*. Although these may be a matter more of mundane belief for some (and hence more in the category of *legend* than *myth*), for others, there are sacred notions attached. Mythic stories of interplanetary travel and various alien races are not confined to fringe systems: rather, many newer religions make reference to extraterrestrial beings. According to the theology of the Latter-day Saints (Mormons), the Garden of Eden was another planet; Jehovah resides on the planet (or perhaps star) Kolob, and there are references to other worlds, with alien races, also created by Jehovah. Somewhat similarly, the more recently begun Scientology offers a detailed origin story of interplanetary travel, warfare, and intrigue, in which our daily lives continue to play a part (the founder of Scientology, L. Ron Hubbard, first became known as a science fiction writer). Other groups, such as the Raëlians, focus squarely on alien belief as the main tenet of their belief system. Many people believe in both biblical and alien stories, syncretizing them into a coherent belief system (as per Erich von Däniken's influential book *Chariots of the Gods*, which reinterprets biblical passages in terms of alien beliefs: in this work, "angels" become largely synonymous with "aliens"). "Ancient aliens" mythic beliefs have been increasingly moving from fringe to mainstream (particularly in the United States), with more and more people incorporating aspects of this into their sacred beliefs.

What to make of such emergent mythologies? How can tracking how people develop new mythological traditions, and/or new syncretizations, help us understand the process of mythology? In questions such as these, there remains a great deal of room for mythological research in the contemporary sense, in trying to keep track of the ever-changing world of mythology and mythic belief systems.

Myth Studied Alive

Myths are some of our most enduring cultural constructions, and the study of myths is one of our oldest theoretical inquiries. Myths attempt to answer the big questions in life: Who am I? What is my relationship to the wider world? Why am I here? What is it to be a good person/man/woman/parent/citizen? Why is the world shaped in the way it is? What happens when we die? The answers to these questions have been put in symbolic form in a wide range of narratives, exemplifying the richness of human diversity. Such "big questions" lie at the heart of the human condition, and have been perennially pondered, performed, and reworked in countless iterations from untold generations. To understand mythology is to understand the vast human potential in imagining explanations of the most mysterious, and the most inscrutable.

Myths are deeply embedded in differing systems of linguistic and cultural symbolism, both lodged in and reflecting particular and distinct worldviews. As we have noted, this embeddedness has at times made it difficult for scholars to lift the subject out of its own existence, and into the realm of philosophical research. The "axes of comparison" set out in chapter 3 suggested some general parameters by which mythologies can be described, analyzed, and compared with other mythologies. These "axes" derive from and point to qualities, patterns, and orientations manifest in or implied by mythic narrative texts themselves; and it is important to understand that the content of such narratives has provided the focus of most systematically comparative myth study thus far.

But we have also called attention in chapter 2 to new issues opened up by the study of myths in their living contexts as dramatized and championed by the anthropologist Bronisław Malinowski, who claimed to have the "myth-maker" at his elbow as well as "a host of authentic commentators to draw upon." Malinowski was not beyond methodological chauvinism; moreover, recent historical analysis of his own work has thrown some doubt on the extent to which he himself was able to implement the participatory immersion in living context that his polemical writings advocate. Also, it must be acknowledged that the opportunity to participate in a group with an active myth-telling tradition is in many cases simply not available to the student of myth, most obviously in instances in which the tradition under investigation is confined to the historical past (how much will we ever truly know of all the everyday ways in which ancient Sumerians participated in the myths?).

The issues opened up by Malinowski, and by subsequent investigators who were and are able to study myth in living context, offer ideals that students of myth should be aware of and strive to implement to whatever extent possible; and thus we choose to draw our introduction to the study of myth to a close around this theme. When direct observation of and participation in living contexts is not possible, it may still be possible and profitable to construct or reconstruct aspects of context from the internal content of mythic texts, from other related texts or contextual evidence, from historical and/or ethnographic studies of the societies in question, or even through ethnographic analogies drawn from similar societies (though of course such analogies necessarily remain somewhat speculative).

The following questions summarize some main aspects or parameters of living context that students should keep in mind and attempt to address in whatever way and to whatever extent possible. Complementing the "points to keep in mind" presented in chapter 3, these parameters continue to offer more tools for the toolkit for approaching, characterizing, comparing, and attempting to develop a sensitive and informed understanding of the world's mythologies.

How Are the Myths Performed?

There are a great variety of ways in which myths are instantiated by people. The performance of myth may well involve or require particular aesthetic styles, devices, and/or expository skills and strategies. Among these may be gestural and other motor techniques, mimetic patterns, vocal skills, mnemonic devices, and a host of other dimensions and realms through which human creativity and imagination find expression. Performances may be governed by the strictest rules of conformity to established patterns or may offer opportunities for virtuosic display and/or improvisation.

Through What Media Are Myths Conveyed?

Even by our narrow definition of myths as narratives, we may notice that some cultures place their myths primarily in written contexts, while others give primacy to orality. Myths may at times be encoded into material culture, from pottery and tapestries to clothing and tattoos. Stories, music, dance, tattooing, hunting, gathering, reaping, sowing, jokes, and comic books... all of these, as well as combinations of them, may be ways that people learn and perform the mythic narratives.

Who Tells the Myths?

Some myths may be related primarily by a select group of people—priests, holy men, bards, etc.—or they may be recounted by nearly everyone. There may be attitudes of "ownership" toward myths. Are the myths in question common, official myths of a nation-state or ethnic group? Minority or persecuted religious voices? Myths of other forms of belonging? Which group or groups tells the myth, and who are they? How are rights and responsibilities associated with a mythic tradition distributed within a particular society? We may also ask, what is the role of the scholar in telling myths? What problems might this imply, as the line between scholar of myths, and myth-maker, can become blurred?

Do Different Variants of Particular Narratives Exist?

What is the nature of variation within the society and myth tradition in question? Do variations relate to the interests or competitive claims of particular individuals or subgroups? Is variation accepted, or is there a feeling that one version must be correct and/or a desire to reconcile varying narrative claims? Who, if anyone, has the right to attempt such reconciliations?

Who Are the Audiences, and What Is Their Role?

How are appropriate audiences defined? Are there restrictions on who should hear or have access to particular narratives? Are hearers/readers expected to passively absorb, or to actively participate in the imparting of myths? Are they allowed or expected to critique the teller or writer of the narrative? What social norms govern the interaction of teller and audience?

In What Contexts Are Myths Told or Produced?

In the mid-to-late twentieth century, anthropologist Dell Hymes (1974) spearheaded a movement, known as the "ethnography of speaking," which called for close observational studies of culturally recognized "events" or "occasions" of speaking. The text—that is, what is actually said—is one part of a speaking event, but Hymes emphasized the critical importance of numerous other dimensions of such events, especially those relating to the specific contexts in which speaking takes place. For example, what are the spatial parameters of recognized speaking events? What are the temporal parameters (for example, are myths imparted only during certain seasons or during certain rituals)? What is the expected psychological mood or tone?

What Are the Immediate or Situated Consequences of Telling/Producing of Myths?

For example, does the beginning of a myth narration alter the tone or mood of a gathering? Does it invite ancestral or spiritual presences? Some linguists use the term "speech act" to call attention to the fact that "saying" often amounts to a "doing"—the very saying of something changes the condition of the world that teller and hearer inhabit.

What Categories and Relationships Do the Myths Imply, and What Is Their Relationship to the World of Ordinary Life?

Myths often lay out the fundamental categories that define a particular way of life, delineating the basic physical, moral, and metaphysical entities, qualities, and relationships that make up the cosmos. Does the telling/producing affirm structure and/or relationships, for example, religious, political, familial, genealogical, gender, and so forth? Formation of gender, marriage, and sexuality are perennial favorites in mythology, as they, like mythology, are universally found core concepts in all human societies. Other cultures may include other important cultural themes, such as desirable or undesirable personality traits, moieties, fate, or the like.

On the other hand, some categories and relationships that occur in myths seem to be mostly internal to myths, raising the question of the relation between the world inside myth and the world outside. In such cases, one must ask, in what ways does myth reflect ordinary life, and in what ways does it alter or distort it—and what are the possible reasons for such alterations/distortions? Vis-à-vis the ordinary world, does the world inside seem myth continuous, permeable, and/or accessible, or does it appear to be sealed and self-contained? If the latter, are there ways in which the world inside can be accessed? Ritually? Through dreams? Vision quests? Divination?

What Wider Roles Does the Myth Play in the Culture and Society?

As is probably becoming increasingly evident, the context of a living myth ultimately amounts to the full life of the society in which it occurs. Thus, the fuller one's understanding is of the society in which a myth occurs, the better one is positioned to appreciate any myth's significance. Are we talking about a society of hunter-gatherers? Then, what do they hunt and gather? And where, and how? It is no great surprise that the Inuit goddess Sedna lives at the bottom of the ocean, from where she sends, or withholds, game to the upper world. The Inuit are primarily a maritime society, relying heavily on the sea for their protein-rich diet. Or is the society largely farmers? What do they farm? The Corn Goddess is a staple divinity, just as corn (maize) was a staple crop, for many Native American groups. In the Abrahamic tradition, humans are commanded by God to become farmers, after being cast out of the garden of Eden. And how do they farm? Is it a water-rich environment, or a dry one? The Hindu rice farmers of Bangladesh place importance on the unfired clay sculptures that house their divinities during annual ritual events, and which are returned to the water after the rituals, recalling the importance of the mineral-rich waters that flood down from the Himalayas, enriching their soil.

Times of great change are particularly interesting in the way that older myths can be changed, or reinterpreted, to provide new meaning in new contexts. For example, the ancestral totemic deity of the Mt. Kare python in Papua New Guinea has been reinterpreted as the provider of gold, and the progenitor of the new gold mining industry which has swept through the land, wreaking great economic and social changes (see Biersack 1999). In the Bikini islands, the trickster god Letao is said to be behind the atomic bombs, and the transformations made by the colonial military force of the United States (see McArthur 2008). In other situations, older mythic stories might be forgotten, or demoted into non-sacred tales for children, or perhaps hybridized with colonial mythic narratives.

What Is the Relationship between the Mythic System under Consideration and Other Mythic Systems?

Does the content and/or context of a particular myth suggest interactions with other mythic traditions? Are there historical connections or influences? Is there duress or pressure, such as colonial impositions? Is there syncretism, or blending of traditions? Is the interaction oppositional (e.g., the other side is "wrong" or "evil")? How has the mythological tradition changed over time, and does our data set allow us to glimpse this process? If it does, what sorts of changes took or are taking place, and what remains the same? Have the mythic narratives undergone translation, or translations? If so, how can we best grasp the myth in the original linguistic context, as well as understand the transformations it has undergone?

Ideally, one would combine these performative questions with the more atemporal, conceptual ones as posed in chapter 3's "axes of comparison" (concerning such concepts as *time, space, quantity, quality,* and *relation*). An examination of such interrelations between the performed and the conceptual can help illuminate how myths interact with everyday life in ways both quotidian and extraordinary.

In direct contradiction to earlier scholars who saw myth as doomed to recede before the superior discourse of science, we may note that myths continue to play an active role in the world today. Mythology is, then, a subject of great antiquity, and also of our contemporary lives. Mythology continues to give meaning to people around the world, and studying the processes by which people continually mythologize and re-mythologize holds great potential toward understanding humanity and human cultures.

Conclusion

Moving Forward with Myth

Asking Questions

The questions covered in this text are opening ones, to help the student and/or researcher better contextualize both the mythic tradition in question, and the relationship between the mythic tradition and myths, generally. They are also geared toward helping the researcher evaluate the data set, and guide further inquiries into various aspects of the society in question.

The most helpful approaches will depend on what interests the researcher: with such a complex phenomenon as mythology, there are plenty of research questions to ask. Perhaps the researcher is interested in language, and the links between mythology and language in a particular context. Or perhaps the researcher is more interested in psychology, or rituals, or gender roles, or any number of aspects of human existence. Indeed, as mythology plays such a fundamental role in cultures, nearly any question regarding human culture and society could be investigated via the role of mythology. If grand, totalizing explanations of mythology seem out of reach, this should not be a cause for despair, but rather an acknowledgment of the complexity of the human condition, and the power of culture in shaping our thoughts, desires, philosophies, and everyday life. It is also an opportunity to use a large repertoire of scholarly mythological approaches toward understanding these fundamental questions. In the end, the goal of all humanities and social science research is self-awareness as encultured beings, whether one is investigating one's own traditions, or foreign ones, or the relations between the two. Toward this goal of understanding ourselves and others, mythology provides a powerful resource.

As we have seen in the historical section, many theories have been proposed for understanding mythology, and many of these have some efficacy. Yet, one of the more common fundamental flaws was to assume that any one explanation was a total explanation for all mythologies, everywhere. Combining these two statements, then, we can state that there are many aspects to the complex phenomenon of mythology and, depending on the mythology and on the questions the researcher wants to answer, many approaches that can be helpful.

Throughout this text, we have covered many approaches and theories. When researching a specific mythology, the researcher might consider which approaches and theories will be most enlightening for the research question at hand. At times, for example in many Chinese folk traditions, the euhemerist approach is eminently plausible and helpful, showing how great leaders or heroes have become increasingly deified, while in other mythological traditions the euhemerist approach may have little or nothing to add to the conversation. Likely, a singular approach will not satisfy by itself: although many Chinese folk traditions can be described as euhemerist, there is much more going on than "simply" (mis-)remembering past heroes: such traditions interact with ongoing philosophical strains of Confucianism and respect for ancestral figures; they often are celebrated with spectacular, and at times intensely local, rituals; they interact with other mythic narratives and traditions in creating a satisfying sacred narrative; and they reflect cultural concerns, linguistic categories, belief systems, and other factors involved in individual and social life.

To recap some of the various productive ways that scholars have investigated mythology: myths are often employed, like science, as a way of understanding the physical environment in which we live. This can range from cosmos in its largest sense to the most intimate relations between specific plants. Yet, myths are often employed, unlike science, as a way to bring meaning to the lives of individuals, connecting us with spiritual forces, whether these are anthropomorphic deities, ancestors, or spirit guides. Myths do function in diverse ways, from organizing societies (as per Malinowski) toward setting up fundamental categories of personhood (as per Wundt, Freud, and Lévi-Strauss). Myths are often strongly connected with rituals (as per Frazer, Smith, and Harrison), yet at times rituals and myths can live somewhat separated lives, as well.

Some of the most compelling newer ethnographic works on mythology may claim an intellectual heritage to a number of competing early outlooks and theories; and discovering how a particular case study reveals particular mythic forces at work has opened up new fields of understanding how mythology works, both similarly and differently, in traditions around the world.

Final Thoughts

Myths make the world, if taken literally. But myths also make the world, taken figuratively: we live in a world of myth-making humans. While the various visions described may at times seem fantastical and strange, familiarity with the societies in question shows instead how the fantastical and strange can come to be seen as part of the normal fabric of life, even within our own traditions, and our own selves. Not only do myths make the world, but they do so in fascinating, and often wildly different, ways. From the muskrat emerging from the watery depths with the first pawful of earth, to the rising up of the gods against the Titans, myths are all in the same employ, yet display at the same time the sublime diversity of human responses to the human condition.

As in our early discussion of Greek mythology, it is not only the myths themselves that provide the most clues in a quest for enlightenment, but also the questions that we ask of myths, questions that reveal not only a march of scholarly research, but also reflect the ever-changing *Zeitgeist* in which myth is queried. In a time of rapid globalization and shrinking of cultural barriers, myths have been brought together at a rapid pace, along with the various diverse peoples influenced by them. The study of myths is, after all, a study of people, a particular *logos* of *anthropos*.

In terms of our planet, this may be a particularly poignant and powerful time to be embarking on such studies: with more potential access to the diversity of human cultures across the globe, humanity is also faced with the consequences of such a scenario. New times require new paradigms, and the study of mythology provides an excellent opportunity for sustained intercultural learning, surely an important aspect of learning to live together in the newly emerging global village. Although often thought of as a past-oriented topic and subject, close analysis reveals rather that myths and myth-making are contemporaneous cultural constructions, constantly being revised, changed, and even newly invented. The future of mythology will depend a great deal on the future of human civilization and culture. And, we would propose, the reverse is likely true as well.

GLOSSARY

animism—the practice of attributing life (and/or souls) to inanimate objects.

anthropocentrism—the assumption that humans are the center of the cosmos, either spatially or in terms of the purpose of the cosmos (so that the other entities of the cosmos are thought to exist *for us*).

anthropomorphism—the practice of attributing human form or characteristics (especially the capacity for thoughts and feelings) to non-human objects.

archetype—broadly, any cross-culturally recurrent mythic idea, image, or pattern. *Archetype* is also used more narrowly to specify the theory proposed by the psychologist C. G. Jung that the human mind contains an unconscious region (the "collective unconscious") comprising such universal archetypes, and that these can be discovered through the cross-cultural study of mythology, dreams, and art.

armchair research—academic slang for research that is limited to books or other sources disseminated through writing; the term is often used derogatorily by those who argue that the study of mythology and culture is better carried on through attendance at and observation of actual myth performances and of the broader societies in which these occur.

chthonic—deriving from the early Greek god Chthonos, who dwelled underground, chthonic deities are those located deep within the earth, often paired with both life and death and temporally mapped onto agricultural seasons.

collective unconscious—see **archetype**

comparative mythology—broadly, any study of mythology from a comparative or cross-cultural perspective. More narrowly, comparative mythology can designate the comparative study of different mythologies within one language family (most commonly, the Indo-European family).

cosmogony—the part of cosmology focused specifically on the *origin* of the cosmos.

cosmology—theories, portrayals, or the study of the **cosmos**.

cosmos—originally, that part of the cosmos which is subject to human or humanizable order (typically surrounded by disorder or chaos). In modern scientific contexts, *cosmos* has come to mean, rather, the totality of the universe as a physical system.

culture hero—a mythic protagonist who brings culture to humans, allowing human groups to distinguish themselves from other natural species and/or from other human groups. The gifts of culture heroes span both technology (e.g., fire, bow-and-arrow) and intellectual/artistic knowledge and skills (such as social or aesthetic values or rules).

cyclical time—time thought of, or experienced, as a continuous returning to the same point (as in the daily, weekly, or yearly round).

degenerationism—a perspective that argues or assumes that the course of human history is one of overall decline; in some cases, the opposite of **evolutionism**.

demigod—a mythic figure who is half god, usually as a result of mixed divine-human parentage.

dissemination—the process of narrative or cultural elements spreading through a geographical region, whether through migration or communication between adjacent peoples; similar to *diffusion*.

emergence myth—a mythic narrative format, associated especially with the North American Southwest, in which humans arrive to the present surface of the earth via a journey from worlds below.

epic—a narrative genre, often originating in oral tradition, which depicts the extraordinary historical achievements of mainly human heroes (although mythological pantheons are often mentioned in the course of the narration of such human adventures). Epics are typically long, artistic works in poetic meter; some amount to historical legends raised to major works of verbal art. The *Iliad* and the *Odyssey* are the best-known epics of Western verbal art.

eschatology—cosmological ideas, images, or narratives pertaining to the final times, such as those comprised in Norse Ragnarök or Christian Apocalypse.

euhemerism—the theory (stemming from fourth/third-century BCE Greek thinker Euhemerus) that mythical stories originated through a process of real, historical individuals or events coming to be exaggerated and dramatized over time.

ex nihilo—literally "from nothing" (Latin); designates theories or portrayals in which the coming-to-be of new things implies no antecedent form or matter; the term **creation** sometimes connotes *ex nihilo*, contrasting on this point with the term **transformation**.

folklore—performed cultural genres that are learned in informal, or face-to-face, settings (as opposed to institutions, or authored literature). Narrowly, the range of artistic genres (e.g., tale, proverb, joke, riddle, songs, dance); more broadly, the range of genres and traditional knowledge and skills (such as quilt-making and home remedies) that circulate through informal channels.

functionalism—a social science perspective (developed especially by sociologist Émile Durkheim and anthropologist Bronisław Malinowski) that emphasizes not the semantic content of cultural products, but rather their consequences within societies and individuals; functionalists often look for the ways in which particular customs serve to maintain the structure and order of the society in which they occur.

geomythology—mythology that includes past geological processes; this is especially notable in long-settled and indigenous cultures. The term may also refer to the scholarly study of such mythology.

hero—the chief protagonist(s) in myth or other narratives, generally designating those protagonists whose achievements have positive consequences for their societies.

historic-geographic method—a method of folklore analysis that focuses on the areal spread of folklore over time, often put to use in a search of origins.

illo tempore—literally *in that time* (Latin); used by scholar of comparative religion Mircea Eliade to call attention to any historical event singled out within a religious tradition as deserving of ongoing ritual return or re-enactment.

legend—an oral narrative that tells of unusual and/or extraordinary adventures or achievements in historical, human time.

liminal—that which escapes binary classifications, resting at the "in-between" of categorical definitions of time, space, and other qualities.

linear time—time thought of, or experienced as, a sequence of non-repeating moments or intervals.

microcosm/macrocosm—paired terms that point to parallel structures at different scales. If an athletic game reflects larger social values, it may be said to be a microcosm of the society (the macrocosm) in which it occurs.

moiety system—a form of social organization in which the members of a society (and sometimes all entities of the cosmos) are divided into two complementary, exchanging subgroups (or *moieties*).

monogenesis—the idea that a geographically widespread narrative originated a single time and then spread outward; opposite of **polygenesis**.

monomyth—originally coined by James Joyce, popularized by Joseph Campbell as the idea that there is one basic myth, that of the hero's journey.

myth—a narrative of profound, symbolic, or even sacred significance, most commonly appearing as some form of origin story.

myth-ritualism—a school of mythological scholarship, flourishing in the first half of the twentieth century, that emphasizes the close interrelationship of myth and ritual, often taking the position that myths emerged from rituals.

numinous—refers to uncanny, spiritual, religious, transcendent, or otherwise awe-inspiring qualities and experiences.

philology—a historically focused study of language in textual sources, often with the goal to determine earlier or original accounts. The widespread use of philology in Christianity (to determine earlier versions of gospels) influenced nascent studies of folklore and mythology in Europe as well.

polygenesis—the idea that a geographically widespread narrative arose independently multiple times through the area of its distribution; opposite of **monogenesis**.

ritual—a set of prescribed actions or performances, typically cyclical, that dramatize important religious or cultural truths.

sacred/profane—a dichotomy describing the inclusion or absence of the numinous or transcendent (in contrast to the "ordinary"); myths are commonly viewed as "sacred" and, therefore, of heightened importance.

social evolutionism—a dominant perspective in eighteenth- and nineteenth-century social thought, which argued that human societies develop through regular, predictable, progressive stages such as savagery, barbarism, and civilization.

solar mythology—a school of myth theory, prominent in the second half of the nineteenth century, that argued that myths arose from an archaic human poetic rapture at the sight of the sun, moon, and other celestial bodies.

structuralism—the approach of trying to study mythology via structural concerns: these can be based on narrative structures (syntagmatic structuralism), categorical structures (paradigmatic structuralism, the type commonly associated with Claude Lévi-Strauss's work), and/or social structures.

taboo—derived from a Polynesian term, taboo is an ultimate or sacred restriction on a group or individual.

tale—sometimes referred to as "folktale": an oral narrative genre thought of as fictional, told for entertainment, and defined by a mixture of human characters and unusual or supernatural beings, often helpers, such as talking animals or fairies; typically set in indefinite time ("once upon a time"). Little Red Riding Hood and Cinderella are examples of folk tales.

totem—a revered emblem, often representing an ancestral figure of a particular lineage.

transformation—sometimes used by mythologists to distinguish origin stories that portray the coming-to-be of present reality as a *re-shaping* of pre-existing matter and/or forms, rather than as an *ex nihilo creation*.

transformer—a mythical protagonist who brings about the present world through **transformation;** less often, a protagonist capable of shape-shifting.

trickster—a type of mythological protagonist characterized by mischievous conduct and/or ambiguous or contradictory qualities (e.g., wise and foolish, young and old, selfish and altruistic).

variant—a different version of recognizably the same story.

worldview—a total view of the cosmos and life within it; some scholars look for a theme or themes that permeates all aspects of the life and thought of a particular society or individual.

WORKS CITED

Babcock-Abrahams, Barbara. 1975. "'A Tolerated Margin of Mess.'" *Journal of the Folklore Institute* 11: 147–86.

Bachofen, Johan. 1861. *Das Mutterrecht: eine Untersuchung über die Gynaikokratie der alten Welt nach ihrer religiösen und rechtlichen Natur.* Stuttgart: Verlag von Krais und Hoffmann.

Bakhtin, M. M. 1982. *The Dialogic Imagination*. Austin: University of Texas Press.

Barber, Elizabeth, and Paul Barber. 2004. *When They Severed Earth from Sky*. Princeton: Princeton University Press.

Barthes, Roland. 1986. *The Rustle of Language*. New York: Hill and Wang.

Barthes, Roland. 1995. *Mythologies*. New York: Hill and Wang.

Bascom, William. 1954. "Four Functions of Folklore." *Journal of American Folklore* 67: 333–49.

Basso, Keith H. 1988. "'Speaking with Names': Language and Landscape among the Western Apache." *Cultural Anthropology* 3: 99–130

Basso, Keith H. 1989. "Stalking with Stories: Names, Places, and Moral Narratives Among the Western Apache." In *Western Apache Language and Culture*, 99–137. Tucson: University of Arizona Press.

Becker, Ernest. 1973. *The Denial of Death*. New York: Simon & Schuster.

Becker, Ernest. 1975. *Escape from Evil*. New York: Free Press.

Beckwith, Martha Warren, ed. 1986. *The Kumulipo: A Hawaiian Creation Chant*. Honolulu: University of Hawaii Press.

Benedict, Ruth. 1934. *Zuni Mythology*. 2 vols. Contributions to Anthropology 21. New York: Columbia University Press.

Best, Elsdon. 1976. *Maori Religion and Mythology, Part I*. rev. ed. Wellington: Government Printer.

Biersack, Aletta. 1999. "The Mount Kare Python and His Gold: Totemism and Ecology in the Papua New Guinea Highlands." *American Anthropologist* 101: 68–87.

Boas, Franz. 1905–1906. "The Mythologies of the Indians." *The International Quarterly* 11: 327–42; 12: 157–73.

Boas, Franz. 1916. *Tsimshian Mythology*. 31st Annual Report of the Bureau of American Ethnology. Washington, DC: Government Printing Office.

Briffault, Robert. 1931 (original 1927). *The Mothers: The Matriarchal Theory of Social Origins*. New York: Macmillan.

Brisson, Luc. 2004. *How Philosophers Saved Myths*. Chicago: University of Chicago Press.

Brown, Michael. 2003 *Who Owns Native Culture?* Cambridge: Harvard University Press.

Burkert, Walter. 1983. *Homo Necans: The Anthropology of Ancient Greek Sacrificial Ritual and Myth*. Berkeley: University of California Press.

Campbell, Joseph. 1959. *The Masks of God*. New York: Viking Press.

Campbell, Joseph. 1968. *The Hero with a Thousand Faces*, Princeton, NJ: Princeton University Press.

Carey, John. 1999. *A Single Ray of the Sun: Religious Speculation in Early Ireland*. Andover: Celtic Studies Publications.

Cormier, Loretta. 2006. "A Preliminary View of the Neotropical Primates in the Subsistence and Symbolism of Indigenous Lowland South American Peoples." *Ecolological and Environmental Policy* 2: 14–32.

Courlander, Harold. 1971. *The Fourth World of the Hopis*. Albuquerque: University of New Mexico Press.

Courlander, Harold. 2002. *A Treasury of African Folklore: The Oral Literature, Traditions, Myths, Legends, Epics, Tales, Recollections, Wisdom, Sayings, and Humor of Africa*. New York: Marlowe & Company.

Cullon, Deirdre. 2013. "A View from the Watchman's Pole: Salmon, Animism, and the Kwakwaka'wakw Summer Ceremonial." *BC Studies* 177: 9–37.

Cushing, Frank Hamilton. 1965. "The Cock and the Mouse." In *The Study of Folklore*, edited by Alan Dundes, 269–76. Englewood Cliffs, NJ: Prentice Hall.

Dégh, Linda. 2001. *Legend and Belief: Dialectics of a Folklore Genre*. Bloomington: Indiana University Press.

Deloria, Vine, Jr. 1995. *Red Earth White Lies*. New York: Scribner.

Doniger O'Flaherty, Wendy. 1988. *Other People's Myths*. Chicago: University of Chicago Press.

Dooley, Anne, and Harry Roe. Trans. 1999 (origin. c. 1200). *Tales of the Elders of Ireland (Acallam na Sénorach)*. New York: Oxford University Press.
Douglas, Mary. 2002. *Purity and Danger*. Florence: Routledge.
Dundes, Alan. 1968. "The Number Three in American Culture." In *Every Man His Way: Readings in Cultural Anthropology*, edited by Alan Dundes, 401–24. Englewood Cliffs, NJ: Prentice Hall.
Dundes, Alan. 1988. *The Flood Myth*. Berkeley: University of California Press.
Dundes, Alan. 2005. "Folkloristics in the Twenty-first Century (AFS Invited Presidential Plenary Address, 2004)." *Journal of American Folklore* 118: 385–408.
Eisler, Riane. 1987. *The Chalice and the Blade: Our History, Our Future*. New York: HarperCollins.
Eliade, Mircea. 1969. *The Two and the One*. New York: Harper and Row.
Eliade, Mircea. 2005. *The Myth of the Eternal Return*. Princeton: Princeton University Press.
Firth, Raymond. 1984. "The Plasticity of Myth: Cases from Tikopia." In *Sacred Narrative*, edited by Alan Dundes, 207–16. Berkeley: University of California Press.
Frazer, James George. 1900. *The Golden Bough: A Study in Magic and Religion*. London: Macmillan.
Frazer, James George. 1988. *Folklore in the Old Testament*. New York: Avenel.
Gardner, Gerald. 1954. *Witchcraft Today*. London: Rider.
Gimbutas, Marija. 1965. *Bronze Age Cultures of Central and Eastern Europe*. The Hague: Mouton.
Gimbutas, Marija. 1974. *The Gods and Goddesses of Old Europe, 7000 to 3500 BC; Myths, Legends, and Cult Images*. London: Thames & Hudson.
Gimbutas, Marija. 1989. *The Language of the Goddess: Unearthing the Hidden Symbols of Western Civilization*. San Francisco: Harper & Row.
Gimbutas, Marija. 1991. *The Civilization of the Goddess: The World of Old Europe*. San Francisco: Harper San Francisco.
Girard, René. 1987. *Things Hidden since the Foundation of the World*. Redwood City, CA: Stanford University Press.
Girard, René. 1989. *The Scapegoat*. Baltimore: Johns Hopkins University Press.
Glassie, Henry. 2002. "Mud and Mythic Vision: Hindu Sculpture in Modern Bangladesh." In *Myth: A New Symposium*, edited by Gregory Schrempp and William Hansen, 203–22. Bloomington: Indiana University Press.
Gomme, Laurence. 1908. *Folklore as an Historical Science*. London: Methuen & Co.

Gottlieb, Alma. 1986. "Dog: Ally or Traitor? Mythology, Cosmology, and Society among the Beng of Ivory Coast." *American Ethnologist* 13: 477–88.
Graves, Robert. 1955. *The Greek Myths*. Baltimore: Penguin.
Grey, George. 1855. *Polynesian Mythology*. London: John Murray.
Griaule, Marcel. 1970 (1965). *Conversations with Ogotemmêli: An Introduction to Dogon Religious Ideas*. Oxford: Oxford University Press.
Grimm, Jacob. 1835. *Deutsche Mythologie*. Göttingen: Dieterichsche Buchhandlung.
Grimm, Jacob, and Wilhelm Grimm. 1816 and 1818. *Deutsche Sagen* (German Legends). Berlin: Der Nicolaischen Buchhandeln.
Grimm, Jacob, and Wilhelm Grimm. 1890. *Fünfzig Kinder- und Hausmärchen*. Leipzig: P. Reclam.
Hafstein, Valdimar. 2009. "Intangible Heritage as a List: From Masterpieces to Representation." In *Intangible Heritage*, edited by Laurajane Smith and Natsuko Akagawa, 93–111. New York: Routledge.
Handy, E. S. C., and E. G. Handy. 1972. *Native Planters in Old Hawaii*. Honolulu: Bishop Museum Press.
Hansen, William. 2009. "Poverty of Cause in Mythological Narrative." *Folklore* 120: 241–52.
Hauser, M., N. Chomsky, and W. T. Fitch. 2002. "The Language Faculty: What Is It, Who Has It, and How Did It Evolve?" *Science* 298: 1569–79.
Hesiod. 1985. *Theogony*. Introduction by Norman O. Brown. Indianapolis: Bobbs-Merrill.
Hill, Jonathan. 2008. *Made-from-Bone: Trickster Myths, Music, and History from the Amazon*. Champaign: University of Illinois Press.
Hyman, Stanley Edgar. 1958. "The Ritual View of Myth and the Mythic." In *Myth: A Symposium*, edited by Thomas Sebeok, 84–94. Bloomington: Indiana University Press.
Hymes, Dell. 1974. *Foundations in Sociolinguistics: An Ethnographic Approach*. Philadelphia: University of Pennsylvania Press.
Hynes, William, and William Doty. 1997. *Mythical Trickster Figures*. Tuscaloosa: University of Alabama Press.
Janet, Pierre. 1928. *L'Évolution de la mémoire et la notion du temps*. Leçons au Collège de France 1927–1928. Paris: Chahine.
Jung, Carl G. 1977. *Mysterium Coniunctionis*. Princeton: Princeton University Press.
Kearney, Michael. 1985. *World View*. Novato: Chandler & Sharp.
Keightley, Thomas. 1828. *The Fairy Mythology*. London: H. Ainsworth.

Kennedy, Lisa. 2008. "'Blood' Hits Gusher of American Myth." *Denver Post* (eEdition, published January 2, 2008; updated May 8, 2016).
Kirk, G. S., J. E. Raven, and M. Schofield. 1983. *The Presocratic Philosophers*. Cambridge: Cambridge University Press.
Krzywinska, Tanya. 2006. "Blood Scythes, Festivals, Quests, and Backstories: World Creation and Rhetorics of Myth in World of Warcraft." *Games and Culture* 1: 383–96.
Lakoff, George. 1987. *Women, Fire, and Dangerous Things*. Chicago: University of Chicago Press.
Leduc, Timothy B. 2010. *Climate Culture Change: Inuit and Western Dialogues with a Warming North*. Ottawa: University of Ottawa Press.
Lévi-Strauss, Claude. 1969. *The Raw and the Cooked*. Harper & Row.
Lévi-Strauss, Claude. 1971. "The Story of Asdiwal." In *The Structural Study of Myth and Totemism*, edited by Edmund Leach, 1–47. London: Tavistock Publications.
Levy, Robert. 1991. *Mesocosm: Hinduism and the Organization of a Traditional Newar City in Nepal*. Berkeley: University of California Press.
Lincoln, Bruce. 1999. *Theorizing Myth: Narrative, Ideology, and Scholarship*. Chicago: University of Chicago Press.
Littleton, C. Scott. 1982. *The New Comparative Mythology: An Anthropological Assessment of the Theories of George Dumézil*. 3rd ed. Berkeley: University of California Press.
Livy. 1985. *The Early History of Rome*. Harmondsworth: Penguin.
Lozada, Lucas Iberico. 2016. "The Professor and the Pueblo: Was the Disclosure of Acoma Traditions Exploitation or Scholarship?" *Santa Fe Reporter* (January 27, 2016). Online at www.sfreporter.com/santafe/article-11510-the-professor-and-the-pueblo.html.
Luomala, Katherine. 1949. *Maui-of-a-Thousand-Tricks: His Oceanic and European Biographers*. Honolulu. Bernice P. Bishop Museum.
Maine, Henry. 1861. *Ancient Law, Its Connection with the Early History of Society, and Its Relation to Modern Ideas*. London: John Murray.
Malinowski, Bronisław. 1992. *Magic, Science, and Religion*. Prospect Heights, IL: Waveland Press.
Mannhardt, Wilhelm. 1875–1877. *Wald- und Feldkulte*. Berlin: Gebrüder Borntraeger.
McArthur, Phillip H. 2008. "Ambivalent Fantasies: Local Prehistories and Global Dramas in the Marshall Islands. " *Journal of Folklore Research* 45: 263–98.

McMillan, A., and I. Hutchinson. 2002. "When the Mountain Dwarfs Danced: Aboriginal Traditions of Paleoseismic Events along the Cascadia Subduction Zone of Western North America." *Ethnohistory* 49: 41–68.

Morgan, Lewis. 1871. *Systems of Consanguinity and Affinity of the Human Family* Washington, DC: Smithsonian Institution.

Mould, Tom. 2002. "Prophetic Riddling: A Dialogue of Genres in Choctaw Performance." *Journal of American Folklore* 115: 395–421.

Murray, Margaret. 1921. *The Witch-Cult in Western Europe*. Oxford: Oxford University Press.

Murray, Margaret. 1931. *The God of the Witches*. London: Faber & Faber.

Nagy, Gregory. 2002. "Can Myth Be Saved?" In *Myth: A New Symposium*, edited by Gregory Schrempp and William Hansen, 240–48. Bloomington: Indiana University Press.

Niles, J. 1999. *Homo Narrans: The Poetics and Anthropology of Oral Literature*. Philadelphia: University of Pennsylvania Press.

Noyes, Dorothy. 2006. "The Judgment of Solomon." *Cultural Analysis* 5: 27–56.

Numazawa, K. 1984. "The Cultural-Historical Background of Myths on the Separation of Sky and Earth." In *Sacred Narrative*, edited by Alan Dundes, 182–92. Berkeley: University of California Press.

Opler, Morris. 1938. *Myths and Tales of the Jicarilla Apache Indians*. New York: American Folklore Society.

Plato. 1971. *Symposium*. Harmondsworth: Penguin.

Porter, Abbott H. *The Cambridge Introduction to Literature*. 2nd ed. Cambridge: Cambridge University Press, 2008.

Puhvel, Jaan. 1987. *Comparative Mythology*. Baltimore: Johns Hopkins University Press.

Pyysiäinen, Ilkka. 1999. "Holy Book: A Treasury of the Incomprehensible. The Invention of Writing and Religious Cognition." *Numen* 46: 269–90.

Radin, Paul. 1950. "The Basic Myth of North American Indians." In *Eranos-Jahrbuch, 1949*, 359–419. Zurich: Rheim-Verlag.

Radin, Paul. 1987. *The Trickster*. New York: Schocken.

Raftery, Barry. 1994. *Pagan Celtic Ireland: The Enigma of the Irish Iron Age*. London: Thames & Hudson.

Raglan, Lord. 1936. *The Hero: A Study in Tradition, Myth, and Drama*. New York: Dover Publications.

Rank, Otto. 1957 (1914). *The Myth of the Birth of the Hero; a Psychological Interpretation of Mythology*. New York: R. Brunner.

Redfield, Robert. 1989. *The Little Community*. Chicago: University of Chicago Press.

Rooth, Anna Birgitta. 1984. "The Creation Myths of the North American Indians." In *Sacred Narrative*, edited by Alan Dundes, 166–81. Berkeley: University of California Press.

Rosaldo, Renato. 1987. "Where Objectivity Lies: The Rhetoric of Anthropology." In *The Rhetoric of the Human Sciences*, edited by John Nelson and Donald McCloskey, 87–110. Madison: University of Wisconsin Press.

Sagan, Carl. 1994. *Pale Blue Dot*. New York: Random House.

Schrempp, Gregory. 1992. *Magical Arrows: The Maori, the Greeks, and the Folklore of the Universe*. Madison: University of Wisconsin Press.

Schrempp, Gregory. 1998. "Distributed Power: A Theme in Native American Origin Stories." In *Stars Above Earth Below*, edited by M. Bol, 15–27. Pittsburgh: Carnegie Museum.

Schwartz, F. L. W. 1860. *Der Ursprung der Mythologie: dargelegt an griechischer und deutscher Sage*. Berlin: W. Hertz.

Segal, Robert. 1984. "Joseph Campbell's Theory of Myth." In *Sacred Narrative: Readings in the Theory of Myth*, edited by Alan Dundes, 256–69. Berkeley: University of California Press.

Shorter, David Delgado. 2009. *We Will Dance Our Truth*. Lincoln: University of Nebraska Press.

Slater, Candace. 2002. "Myths of the Rain Forest/The Rain Forest as Myth." In *Myth: A New Symposium*, edited by Gregory Schrempp and William Hansen, 151–64. Bloomington: Indiana University Press.

Spivak, Gayatri. 1988. "Can the Subaltern Speak?" In *Marxism and the Interpretation of Culture*, edited by Cary Nelson and Lawrence Grossberg, 271–313. Urbana: University of Illinois Press.

Stanner, W. E. H. 1972 [1956]. "The Dreaming." Reprinted in *Reader in Comparative Religion*, edited by William E. Lessa and Evon Z. Vogt, 269–77. 3rd ed. New York: Harper and Row.

Steverlynck, Astrid. 2008. "Amerindian Amazons: Women, Exchange, and the Origins of Society." *Journal of the Royal Anthropological Institute* 14: 572–58.

Stone, Merlin. 1976. *When God Was a Woman*. Original title *The Paradise Papers: The Suppression of Women's Rites*. New York: Barnes and Noble.

Sturluson, Snorri. c. 1220. *The Prose Edda*.

Tedlock, Dennis, ed. 1996. *Popol Vuh*. New York: Touchstone.

Thompson, Stith. 1953. "The Star Husband Tale." *Studia Septentrionalia* 4: 93–163.

Toelken, Barre. 2002. "Native American Reassessment and Reinterpretation of Myths." In *Myth: A New Symposium*, edited by Gregory Schrempp and William Hansen, 89–105. Bloomington: Indiana University Press.

Traube, Elizabeth. 1986. *Cosmology and Social Life*. Chicago: University of Chicago Press.
Turner, Stephanie. 2012. "The Case of the Zia: Looking beyond Trademark Law to Protect Sacred Symbols." Student Scholarship Papers 124. http://digitalcommons.law.yale.edu/student_papers/124.
UN General Assembly, *United Nations Declaration on the Rights of Indigenous Peoples: Resolution Adopted by the General Assembly*, 2 October 2007, A/RES/61/295, available at: http://www.refworld.org/docid/471355a82.html (accessed 25 September 2017).
van der Sluijs, Marinus, and Anthony L. Peratt. 2009. "The Ourobóros as an Auroral Phenomenon." *Journal of Folklore Research* 46: 3–41.
van Gennep, Arnold. 1961. *The Rites of Passage*. Chicago: University of Chicago Press.
Vaz Da Silva, Francisco. 2007. "Folklore into Theory: Freud and Lévi-Strauss on Incest and Marriage." *Journal of Folklore Research* 44: 1–19
Vecsey, Christopher. 1991. *Imagine Ourselves Richly: Mythic Narratives of North American Indians*. New York: HarperCollins.
Vitaliano, Dorothy. 1973. *Legends of the Earth*. Bloomington: Indiana University Press.
von Däniken, Erich. 1968. *Chariots of the Gods*. Original title *Erinnerungen an die Zukunft: Ungelöste Rätsel der Vergangenheit*. New York: Putnam.
White, Hayden. 1987. *The Content of the Form: Narrative Discourse and Historical Representation*. Baltimore: Johns Hopkins University Press.
Wilson, E. O. 1998. *Consilience*. New York: Alfred A. Knopf.
Zolbrod, Paul. 2010. *Diné bahane': The Navajo Creation Story*. Albuquerque: University of New Mexico Press.

INDEX

For the benefit of digital users, indexed terms that span two pages (e.g., 52–53) may, on occasion, appear on only one of those pages.

Aarne, Antti, 64–65
Aarne-Thompson tale type index, 64–65
Abrahamic religions/traditions, 35, 168–69, 175–76
   anthropocentrism, 29–30
   divine in heavens, 33
   dominance, 101
   earth as non-divine, 166
   Flood Myth, 32–33, 108–9
   Frazer on, 59–60
   "God the Father" of, Freud on, 72–73
   heaven and the Bible, 28–29
   origin story, 166
   ownership, 162
   writing and reading, 10
academic discipline, emergence, 47–49
aliens, ancient, 169–70
alive study, 171–76
   audience, 174
   categories and relationships implied, 175
   consequences, immediate/situated, 174
   context, 174
   media, 173
   mythic systems, interrelationships, 176
   narrator, 173
   performance, 172
   roles in society, wider, 175
   variants, narratives, 173
American anthropology (Boas), 66–68
ancient aliens, 169–70
Ancient City, The (de Coulanges), 115–16
Ancient Law (Maine), 85, 96
Ancient Society (Morgan), 85–86
Anderson, Paul Thomas, *There Will Be Blood*, 26
animism, 22

anthropology, 66
  American (Boas), 66–68
  as ethnography
    (Malinowski), 68–70
anthropomorphism, 22
archaic poetry from heavens
  (Müller), 53–54
archetypes, 80–84
  Jungian, 105
archons, 91–92
Aristotle, "Categories," 106
Aryans, 52
audience, 174
axes of comparison,
  comparative mythology,
    106–32, 171
  quality (kind), 126
  quantity (number), 121
  relation/cause, 132
  space, 113
  time, 107

Bachofen, Johann Jakob, *Das Mutterecht*, 85
Bakhtin, Mikhail, 117–18
Bantu myths, 25
Barber, Elizabeth and Paul, *When They Severed Earth from Sky*, 156–57
Barthes, Roland, 9
  "Blue Blood Cruise," 147–48
  Blue Guide, The, 114
  Mythologies, 147–50
  "Myth Today," 148
  "Soap-powders and Detergents," 149
  "The Face of Garbo," 149
  "The Writer on Holiday," 147
Basso, Keith, 90–91, 117

Becker, Ernest
  Denial of Death, The, 74–75
  Escape from Evil, 74–75
Benedict, Ruth, 76–77
Benfey, Theodor, *Panchatantra*, 52
Biersack, Aletta, 114–15
Blue Guide, The (Barthes), 114
Boas, Franz, 66–68, 108–9
  Tsimshian Mythology, 75–76
Briffault, Robert, *The Mothers: The Matriarchal Theory of Social Origins*, 86
Brison, Luc, 42–43
Britain
  Frazer and myth-ritual school, 60–61
  "Great Debates" (Clodd, Gomme, Lang, Frazer), 59–60
  Harrison, Jane, 61
  search for nation's soul, 55–57
  Smith and myth-ritual school, 59–60
Bronze Age Cultures of Central and Eastern Europe (Gimbutas), 87–88
Brothers Grimm, 49–50, 51
Brown, Michael, *Who Owns Native Culture?*, 163–64
Brown, Norman O., 123–24
Burkert, Walter, *Homo Necans: The Anthropology of Ancient Greek Sacrificial Ritual and Myth*, 97–98

Campbell, John Francis, 56
Campbell, Joseph, 82–83, 153–54
  Hero with a Thousand Faces, The, 82–83, 146
  Language of the Goddess, forward, 88
  as universalist and transcendentalist, 82–83

categories, relationships implied, 175
"Categories" (Aristotle), 106
cause, 132
Celtic mythology, 55–56, 59
   Graves, Robert, 87
   MacRitchie, David, 152
   Tolkien, J. R. R., 146–47
Chalice and The Blade: Our History, Our Future, The (Eisler), 88
changes, textual language, 48–49
Chariots of the Gods (von Däniken), 169–70
Christian Church and thought.
   See also Abrahamic religions/traditions
   Christian era, *logos vs. mythos*, 41–43
   microcosm, 80–81
   printing press, 44–45
   Renaissance and Reformation, 43–46
chronotope, 117–18, 121
chthonic mythologies, 111–12
Civilization of the Goddess, The (Gimbutas), 88
Classical mythology, 34–36, 48–49.
   See also specific types
   theories, fresh applications, 92–93
Clodd, Edward, 59
collective unconscious, 81–82
colonial thinking, 157–58
community, mythic thought as, 70–71
comparative mythology, 57–58, 99–140
   axes of comparison, 106–32, 171
   axes of comparison, quality (kind), 126

axes of comparison, quantity (number), 121
axes of comparison, relation/cause, 132
axes of comparison, space, 113
axes of comparison, time, 107
benefits of study of, 99–101
broad sense, 102
Müller, 54–55
narrow sense, 102
sources of examples, 140–43
coniunctio oppositorum, 130–31
consequences, immediate/situated, 174
contemporary mythologies, 168–70
context, 174
Corn Goddess, 175
cosmogonic (cosmogenesis), 132
   Abrahamic, 168
   definition, 25
   Hesiod's *Theogony*, 25, 133–34
   Jicarilla Apache, 127–28
   Maori, 109–10, 134–35
   Plato's Eros, 40–41
   Sky and Earth, 113
cosmology, 10, 14, 16–17, 21, 23–24, 153–54, 163. See also specific types
Coulanges, Fustel de, *The Ancient City*, 115–16
Coyote, 79, 114–15, 133
creativity, 95–96
Critias (Plato), 150–51
cross-cultural comparison. See comparative mythology
Cruikshank, Julie, *Do Glaciers Listen?*, 165
Cullon, Deirdre, 164
cultural diversity, global, 6

culture, mythology and, 27–34
  fantasy and strangeness, 27–28
  knowing the other, 30
  mythic influences, 33
  popular culture, 145–47
  sacred, nature, 28
  study, purpose, 34
culture hero, 108–9
current trends, 144–77
  alive study, 171–76
  audience, 174
  Barthes, mythologies of
    bourgeoisie, 147–50
  categories and relationships
    implied, 175
  consequences, immediate/
    situated, 174
  contemporary/new/emergent
    mythologies, 168–70
  context, 174
  diachronic analyses, 158
  dichotomy, resolving and
    sustaining, 160
  heritage, 161–64
  media, 173
  mythic systems,
    interrelationships, 176
  narrator, 173
  new takes, what really
    happened, 150–60
  performance, 172
  popular culture, 145–47
  roles in society, wider, 175
  sustainability, 164–68
  variants, narrative, 173
cyclical time, 47–49, 107,
  108–9, 110–11

Dante Alighieri, *Divine Comedy*,
  115–16, 137–38

Darwin, Charles, *Origins of the
  Species, The*, 85
Darwinism, 57
  social, 84–85
definitions, myth, 3, 4–5, 7–20
  by contrast, myth *vs.*
    religion, 17–18
  by contrast, myth *vs.* science,
    17–18, 20
  by contrast, storytelling
    genres, 12–16
  by contrast, timeliness, 16
  by contrast, truthiness, 13
  by contrast, two
    dichotomies, 17–20
  core, 7–11
  core, myth, mythology, mythos,
    mythography, 11
  core, writing, 10
de Fontenelle, Bernard Le Bovier, 45
Dégh, Linda, 14
Deloria Jr., Vine, *Red Earth, White
  Lies: Native Americans and the
  Myth of Scientific Fact*, 155–56
demigod, 112
Democritus, 40
Denial of Death, The
  (Becker), 74–75
Descartes, René, 71
Deutsche Mythologie (Grimm), 50
Deutsche Sagen (Grimm), 50
diachronic analyses, 158
dichotomy, resolving and
  sustaining, 160
Diné (Navajo), 90, 103–4
discipline, folklore,
  emergence, 47–49
dissemination, 95–96, 105
distortion, reflection *vs.*, 75–77
distribution, 95–96

Divine Comedy (Dante),
  115–16, 137–38
Divine feminine, 84–86
Do Glaciers Listen?
  (Cruikshank), 165
Douglass, Mary, 85–86
Dreamtime, 16–17, 28–29, 108, 166
Druids, 46, 55–56
Dumézil, Georges, 54–55
  on "Rape of the Sabine," 152–54
Dundes, Alan, 12–13
Durkheim, Émile, 70–71, 106, 152

earth-diver myth, 113, 114, 128–29
eidos, 34–35
Eisler, Riane, *The Chalice and The Blade: Our History, Our Future*, 88
Electra complex, 73
Eliade, Mircea, 83–84, 153–54
emergence myth, 33, 103–4,
  109, 113, 114, 118–19,
  127–28, 168–70
epic, 15
Escape from Evil (Becker), 74–75
eschatology, 110
ethnography, 66
Euhumerus and euhemerism,
  42–43, 150–51
ex nihilo, 138

Fairy Mythology, The
  (Keightley), 55–56
fairy tales, 15
family tree, 102
feminine, Divine, 84–86
Finland (Finnish method),
  historic-geographic
  Krohns, von Sydow, Aarne, 63–65
  Lönnrot, 62–63
Firth, Raymond, 159

flood myths, 45, 90, 105, 108–9
  Abrahamic, 32–33
folklore studies. *See also* Germany,
  folklore studies; *specific types*
  emergence, 47–49
  Germany, rise of, 49–51
founder effect, 95
Frazer, James George, 137–38
  Golden Bough, The, 59–60
  myth-ritual school, 60–61
Freud, Sigmund
  biological drives, repressed, 81–82
  on "God the Father," 72–73
  myth as personhood and
    psychoanalytic school, 72–74
  thought of, extensions, 74–75
  totemism, 57–58
functionalism, 68, 152

Gardner, Gerald, *Witchcraft Today*, 86–87
general trajectory, 110–11
Gennep, Arnold van, 70–71
genre, 27
geomythology, 155
Germany, folklore studies, 49–51
  Brothers Grimm, 49–50, 51
  Mannhardt, Wilhelm, 50–51
  Schwartz, F. L .W., 50–51
Gimbutas, Marija, 87–88
  *Bronze Age Cultures of Central and
    Eastern Europe*, 87–88
  Civilization of the Goddess, The, 88
  *Goddesses and Gods of Old Europe,
    The*, 88
  Language of the Goddess, The, 88
Girard, René, *The Scapegoat*, 97–98
Glassie, Henry, 9, 90
Glomme, Laurence, 59
glossary, 183–87

Goddesses and Gods of Old Europe, The (Gimbutas), 88
goddess movements, 169
God of the Witches, The (Murray), 86–87
Golden Bough, The (Frazer), 59–60
Graves, Robert, 87
Greco-Roman mythology, 34–36, 42–43, 48–49
Greek myths and philosophers, early, 38–41
Grimm, Wilhelm and Jacob, 49–50, 51
Deutsche Mythologie (German Mythology), 50
Deutsche Sagen (German Legends), 50
Kinder- und HausMärchen (Grimm), 49

Harrison, Jane, 61
Herder, Johann Gottfried von, 46–48
heritage, 161–64
hero, 15
  culture, 108–9
  as transformer, 108–9
Hero, The (Raglan), 82–83
hero's journey, 82–83
Hero with a Thousand Faces, The (Campbell), 82–83, 146
Hesiod, *Theogony*, 24–25, 97–98, 122–24, 125, 127, 129, 130, 133–34, 135–36
historical legend, 15
historic-geographic method, Finland Krohns, von Sydow, and Aarne, 63–65
Lönnrot, 62–63

history, mythological
  research, 37–98
  19th c.: colonialism, change, and academic disciplines, 48–49
  20th c.: ethnography, anthropology, sociology, 66
  American anthropology (Boas), 66–68
  anthropology as ethnography (Malinowski), 68–70
  archaic poetry from heavens (Müller), 53–54
  archetypes and collective unconscious (Lévi-Strauss, Campbell, Eliade), 80–84
  Britain, "Great Debates" (Clodd, Gomme, Lang, Frazer), 59–60
  Britain, search for nation's soul (Keightley, Hyde, Campbell, Rhys, Nutt), 55–57
  Christian era: *logos vs. mythos*, 41–43
  Classic theories, fresh applications, 92–93
  Divine feminine (Maine, Bachofen, Morgan, Briffault), 84–86
  Finland: myth, nation, and historic-geographic method (Lönnrot), 62–63
  Freudian thought, extensions (Malinowski, Rank, Becker, Róheim), 74–75
  German folklore studies (Brothers Grimm, Schwartz, Mannhardt), 49–51
  Greek myths and philosophers, early, 38–41

Index

historic-geographic method (Krohns, von Sydow, Aarne), 63–65
ideology (Lincoln, Spivak), 91–92
India: philology and *Ur*-form (Benfey), 52
Indo-European mythology and language (Müller, Dumézil), 54–55
language, speech, and performance (Basso, Hymes), 90–91
monolithism (one theory), 94–98
myth as personhood: psychoanalytic school (Freud), 72–74
mythic thought as community (Durkheim, Lévy-Bruhl), 70–71
myth-ritual school (Smith, Frazer, Harrison), 60–62
New Millennium: testing theories, deepening understanding, 89–90
psychology (Descartes, Locke, Wundt), 71–72
rationale, 93–94
reflecting *vs.* distorting society (Boas, Benedict), 75–77
Renaissance and Reformation (Vico, de Fontanelle, Toland, Voltaire), 43–46
Romanic Nationalism (Herder), 46–48
social evolution and savage survivals (Spencer, Tylor), 57–58

structuralism and morphology (Lévi-Strauss, Propp), 77–80
witches (Murray, Graves, Gimbutas), 86–89
Homo Narrans: The Poetics and Anthropology of Oral Literature (Niles), 8–9
homo necans, 97–98
Homo Necans: The Anthropology of Ancient Greek Sacrificial Ritual and Myth (Burkert), 97–98
Hopis, 34, 109, 118–19, 121–22
How Forests Think (Kohn), 165
humaniqueness, 8–9
humor, in distortion, 35–36
Hyde, Douglas, 55–56
Hyman, Stanley Edgar, "The Ritual View of Myth and the Mythic," 97
Hymes, Dell, 90–91, 174

ideology, myth as, 91–92
illo tempore, 107–8
independent invention, 105
India, philology and *Ur*-form (Benfey), 52
Indo-European mythology and language, 54–55
Inferno (Dante), 137–38
Ionian School, 39
Ireland, Celtic mythology, 55–56, 59, 87, 146–47, 152

Jakobson, Roman, 78
Janet, Pierre, *L'Evolution de la mémoire de temps*, 8–9
Jicarilla Apache, 90–91, 117, 127–28
Journal of American Folklore, 67–68

Jung, Carl, 81–82
  archetypes, 105
  coniunctio oppositorum, 130–31
  as universalist and
    transcendentalist, 82–83

Kalevala (Lönnrot), 62–63
Keightley, Thomas, *The Fairy Mythology*, 55–56
Kennedy, Lisa, 26
kind, 126
Kinder- und HausMärchen (Grimm), 49
kinship
  connections, 135–36
  principle, 156–57
knowing the other, 30
Kohn, Eduardo, *How Forests Think*, 165
Krohn, Julius, 63–64
Krohn, Kaarle, 63–64

Lang, Andrew, 59
language, 90–91. *See also* philology
Language of the Goddess, The (Gimbutas), 88
legends, 169–70
  historical, 15
  timeliness, 16, 17
  truthiness, 13, 14–15
Legends of the Earth (Vitaliano), 155
Lévi-Strauss, Claude, 31, 153–54
  cultural variation, 80–81
  on depletions in
    content, 123–24
  on myths as reflection *vs.*
    distortion, 35–36
  on opposites, sensory
    invocation, 126–27

  Raw and the Cooked, The, 78–79
  structuralism, 77–80
L'Evolution de la mémoire de temps (Janet), 8–9
Levy, Robert, 115–16
Lévy-Bruhl, Lucien, 70–71
liminal, 79
Lincoln, Bruce, 91
linear time, 48–49, 107, 108–10
Livy, 151
Locke, John, on Descartes, 71
logos, 34–35, 40
  of *anthropos*, 181
  Christian Church, 44
  vs. mythos, 41–43
Lönnrot, Elias, 62–63
Luther, Martin, 44–45

MacRitchie, David, 152
magic, 60–61
magical thinking, 75
Maine, Henry, *Ancient Law*, 85, 96
Malinowski, Bronislaw, 68–70, 74, 152, 171–72
Mannhardt, Wilhelm, 50–51
Märchen, 15
matrilineal kinship, 85–86
Mayor, Adrienne, 154–55
media, 145–47, 172
mesocosm, 115–16
microcosm, 80–81
moiety system, 129–30
monogenesis, 105
monolithism (one theory), 94–98
monomyth, 80–81, 82–83
Morgan, Lewis Henry
  Ancient Society, 85–86
  Systems of Consanguinity and Affinity of the Human Family, 85–86
morphology of myth, 77–80

Mothers: The Matriarchal Theory of Social Origins, The (Briffault), 86
Mount Kare Python, 114–15, 176
Müller, (Friedrich) Max
   archaic poetry from heavens, 53–54
   Indo-European mythology and language, 54–55
   solar mythology, 53–54, 94
Murray, Margaret
   God of the Witches, The, 86–87
   The Witch-Cult in Western Europe, 86–87
muthos, 38
   logos and, 40
mythic influences, 33
mythic systems. *See also specific types*
   interrelationships, 176
mythic thought as community (Durkheim, Lévy-Bruhl), 70–71
Myth of the Birth of the Hero, The (Rank), 74–75
mythography, 12, 47–48
Mythologies (Barthes), 147–50
mythology, 47–48. *See also specific types*
   academic discipline, 18
   as dead religions, 18–19
   terminology and uses, 11–12
mythology research and studies. *See also specific topics*
   data set, 5–6
   emergence, 48–49
   history, 37–98 (*see also* history, mythological research)
   worldviews, cultural, 5–6
mythos
   logos vs. (Christian era), 41–43
   terminology and uses, 11–12
myth-ritualism, 60–62, 97

myths. *See also specific topics*
   debunking connotation, 25–26
   dichotomies and oppositions, 6
   fantastical, 2
   global cultural diversity, 6
   vs. religion, 17–18
   terminology and uses, 11–12
   timeliness, 16–17
   truthiness, 13
   understanding, in general, 1–2
   understanding, in particular, 3
   urban, 2
myth *vs.* science, 17–18, 20

narrative, 7–12
   definition, 7–8
   story, 8–9
narrator, 173
Nationalism, Romanic (Herder), 46–48
Navajo, 90, 103–4, 109, 160
new mythologies, 168–70
New Science, The (Vico), 46
Niles, Jack, *Homo Narrans: The Poetics and Anthropology of Oral Literature*, 8–9
number, 121
nursery tales, 15
Nutt, Alfred, 56

Oedipal complex, 73, 74
Oedipal myth, 73–74
O'Flaherty, Wendy Doniger, 41
On Unbelievable Tales (Palaephatus), 40
oral narrative genre, 15
Origins of the Species, The (Darwin), 85
origin story, 73–74
"Out of India Theory," 52

Palaephatus, *On Unbelievable Tales*, 40
Pale Blue Dot (Sagan), 23–24
Panchatantra (Benfey), 52
Peratt, Anthony L., 158
performance, 90–91, 172
personhood, 29–30, 72–74
philology, 48–49
   definition, 52
   India, 52
   reconstructive attempts, 65
Plato, 34–35, 40–42
   Critias, 150–51
polygenesis, 105
popular culture, 145–47
printing press, 44–45
Propp, Vladimir, 80
psychoanalytic school
   Freud, 72–74
   theory, 97–98
psychology, rise of (Descartes, Locke, Wundt), 71–72
Pyysiäinen, Ilka, 10

quality, 126
quantity, 121
questions, asking, 178–80

Raglan, Lord, *The Hero*, 82–83
Rainbow Serpent, 13
Rank, Otto, 74–75, 82–83
   Myth of the Birth of the Hero, The, 74–75
"Rape of the Sabine," Dumézil on, 152–54
rationalists, 20, 24
rationality, early Greece, 40
Raven, 79, 114–15, 133
Raw and the Cooked, The (Lévi-Strauss), 78–79

Red Earth, White Lies: Native Americans and the Myth of Scientific Fact (Deloria), 155–56
reflection *vs.* distortion, of society, 75–77
Reformation, 43–46
relation/cause, 132
religion. *See also* Christian Church and thought
   vs. myth, 17–18
Renaissance and Reformation, 43–46
research, mythological. *See also* mythology research and studies
   history, 37–98 (*see also* history, mythological research)
Rhys, John, 56
"Ritual View of Myth and the Mythic, The" (Hyman), 97
Róheim, Géza, 75
Romanic Nationalism (Herder), 46–48

sacred
   nature in, 28
   writing, 10
Sagan, Carl, *Pale Blue Dot*, 23–24
Sapir, Edward, 72
sati, 91–92
Saussure, Ferdinand de, 78
savage survivals, 57–58
Scapegoat, The (Girard), 97–98
scholarly studies, recent, 89–90
Schwartz, F. L .W., 50–51
science
   Greece, early, 40
   vs. myth, 17–18, 20
Sedna, 28–29
semiotics, 78
sky and earth myth, 113–14, 134–35

Slater, Candace, 149–50
Smith, William Robertson, 60
snake, 29–30, 34
social Darwinism, 84–85
social evolution and savage
    survivals, 57–58
social evolutionism, 94–95, 96
sociology, 66
solar mythology, 53–54, 94
solipsism, 30–31
Sophists, 40
space, 113
space-time, 117–18, 121
speech, 90–91
speech act, 174–75
Spencerism, 57
Spivak, Gayatri, 91–92
Stone, Merlin, *When God Was a Woman*, 88
story, 8–9
storytelling, 8
    genres, 12–17
    Irish, 55–56
structuralism
    Lévi-Strauss, 77–80
    syntagmatic (Propp), 80
studies, folklore, 47–51. *See also* mythology research and studies
Stukeley, William, 46
Sturluson, Snorri, 151
sublimation, 72–73
sustainability, 164–68
syntagmatic structuralism, 80
Systems of Consanguinity and Affinity of the Human Family (Morgan), 85–86

taboo, 25
tales
    timeliness, 16

truthiness, 13, 14, 15
Tate, Henry W., 75–76
Theogony (Hesiod), 24–25, 97–98, 122–24, 125, 127, 129, 130, 133–34, 135–36
There Will Be Blood (Anderson), 26
Thompson, Stith, 64–65
Tikopians, 123–25, 159–60
time, 107
timeliness, 16
Toelken, Barre, 90, 160
Tochmarc Étaíne, 154–55
Toland, John, 45
Tolkien, J. R. R., 146–47
totemism, 29–30, 57–58
traditional ecological knowledge (TEK), 164–65
transformation myths, 108–9
transformer, 108–9
Traube, Elizabeth, 116
trickster figures, 79
Trobriand Islands, 68, 69–70
truth, Greek myths, 38
truthiness, 13
Tsimshian Mythology (Boas), 75–76
Tylor, Edward Burnett, 57–58

unconscious, collective, 81–82
unitary intention, 123
unity of opposites, 85
universalist approach, Max Müller, 53–54
urban myth, 2
ur-form, 52

van der Sluijs, Marinus Anthony, 158
variants, 95–96
    narratives, 173
Vaz da Silva, Francisco, 73–74
Venus, 104

Vico, Giambattista, 45
Vitaliano, Dorothy, *Legends of the Earth*, 155
Voltaire, 45
von Däniken, Erich, *Chariots of the Gods*, 169–70
von Sydow, Carl Wilhelm, 64

Warner, Marina, 149–50
Whale Rider, 145–46
When God Was a Woman (Stone), 88
When They Severed Earth from Sky (Barber), 156–57
Who Owns Native Culture? (Brown), 163–64
Whorf, Benjamin Lee, 72
Wicca, 86–87, 89, 169
Wilson, E. O., 20–21, 24
wish fulfillment, 75

Witchcraft Today (Gardner), 86–87
Witch-Cult in Western Europe, The (Murray), 86–87
witches, 86–89
world creation, 24–27
world of myths, 103
worldview, 138, 139
  cultural, 5–6, 89–90
  myth/mythology, 17–18, 36, 92
  mythos, 11–12
  natural world, indigenous groups, 118–19
  prescientific, 149
  urbanization on, 96
writing, 10
Wundt, Wilhelm, 71–72

Xenophanes, 39

Zuni Mythology (Benedict), 76–77